THE THE AND YOU
A Beginning

BY MARSH CASSADY

MERIWETHER PUBLISHING LTD.
Colorado Springs, Colorado

Meriwether Publishing Ltd., Publisher
Box 7710
Colorado Springs, CO 80933

Editor: Theodore O. Zapel
Typesetting: Susan Trinko
Cover design: Tom Myers
Book design: Beth Tallakson

Library of Congress Cataloging-in-Publication Data

Cassady, Marsh, 1936-
    The theatre and you : a beginning / by Marsh Cassady. -- 1st ed.
      p.   cm.
    Summary: An introduction to the theater, covering such topics as writing a play, choosing a cast, acting techniques, directing, and more.
    ISBN 0-916260-83-6 : $14.95
    1. Theater--Production and direction. 2. Acting. [1. Theater--Production and direction. 2. Acting.] I. Title.
PN2053.C34   1992
    792--dc20
                                           92-14993
                                                      CIP
                                                      AC

To Edee Suslick

ACKNOWLEDGEMENT OF CREDITS

Excerpts from:
We Are, You Are, They Are, Each Man in His Time, The Closing of the Mine, Script Writer, Ties, Christopher Puppy, The Last Vampire, Going Steady — all written by the book's author, Marsh Cassady. Reprinted by permission of playwright.

An excerpt from:
The Twelve Pound Lock by James Barrie. Reprinted from Public Domain.

An excerpt from:
An Enemy of the People reprinted by permission of Charles Scribner's Sons from the *Collected Works of Henrik Ibsen, Volume VIII,* translated by William Archer, © Copyright 1907 Charles Scribner's Sons.

Carwash and *The Tattoo Parlor* appeared originally in *Crazy Quilt.* Reprinted by permission of the author. Performance rights reserved.

An excerpt from:
Riders to the Sea by John Millington Synge. Reprinted from Public Domain.

Excerpts from:
As You Like It and *Two Gentlemen from Verona* by William Shakespeare.

Anniversary by Conrad Bishop and Elizabeth Fuller. © Copyright 1979 C. Bishop and E. Fuller. All public and contest performances are subject to a royalty fee. For permission write Word Workers Press, P.O. Box 1363, Lancaster, PA 17603.

An excerpt from:
The Importance of Being Ernest by Oscar Wilde. Reprinted from Public Domain.

Joan, a play from *Two Characters Plays for Student Actors* by Robert Mauro. © Copyright 1988 Meriwether Publishing Ltd., Colorado Springs, CO 80907. Performance rights reserved.

An excerpt from:
A Thing of Beauty by Charles Kray. Reprinted by permission of the author, July 1991. Performance rights reserved.

Thanks to Peterson Stage Lighting of San Diego, CA for supplying models of various lighting instruments and boards.

PHOTO ACKNOWLEDGMENTS

The Birthday Party, directed by Lynn Bohart at San Diego State University. Used by permission of San Diego State Dramatic Arts Department.

The Lion in Winter, directed and designed by Mary Sesak, Heidelberg College, Tiffin, Ohio. Photo by Jeff McIntosh and used with his permission.

Long Day's Journey Into Night, directed by Bedford Thurman, and *Once Upon a Mattress,* directed by William Zucchero, make-up by Jacque De Cosmo. Photos by James Gleason and used by permission of Kent State University.

Sugar, directed by Jill Lynn, and *A Thurber Carnival,* designed by Rich Jagunic. Photos used by permission of Little Theatre of Tuscarawas County (Ohio).

PUBLISHER'S PREFACE

"What text would you recommend for teaching students acting and stage movement?" . . . "Is there a good book about how to write and stage a play?" . . . "How is real theatre different from TV and films?" . . . "Is there a book that explains the total concept of putting on a stage play?"

These are typical of the many questions asked of our staff at Contemporary Drama Service, a division of our publishing company that has been providing plays, playkits and performance aids to schools nationwide for over 20 years. Our people have done their very best to provide answers and recommendations. But too often the list of suggested books exceeded the budget of the teacher or would-be play producer. Then followed the obvious question: "Isn't there one book that tells it all?"

Until now the answer has been negative. But we perceived the need and accepted the challenge. The answer is in your hand — a book that provides a glimpse into the basics of theatre as a performance art and craft written by a theatre professional who has been playwright, director and actor in staged theatricals of all types. We selected Marsh Cassady to write this book because of his eminence in the field of drama education.

Within the relatively short time that teacher and student have to step into the complex world of theatre, they can only hope to be introduced to the major concepts of each subject. The author has endeavored to develop a comprehensive text in a simplified form that will provide a workable structure for teaching beginning theatre. Our many other books on specialty areas of drama and stagecraft can provide other in-depth study materials as needed.

We hope this book will work well for you.

CONTENTS

PART I
Getting Acquainted with Theatre

PART II
Directing

PART III
Design

PART V
A History of the Theatre

CHAPTER 15

PART I
GETTING ACQUAINTED
WITH THEATRE

CHAPTER ONE
Why Study Theatre?

Theatre can be fun. That is probably the most important reason for learning about it. But there are other reasons. Before seeing what they are, it might be a good idea to figure out exactly what theatre is.

Definition of Theatre

Theatre is an art form, just as painting or sculpture is. It's a way of presenting something that the playwright, actors, director and designers think is important. It's taking this "something" and expressing the thoughts about it in a way that is appealing and significant. This means that theatre, like the other arts, should attract people and interest them. It should be enjoyable or stimulating.

Theatre is one of the oldest art forms. Imagine the following scene:

The Campfire

1
2
3 **CHARACTERS:** OGG, a young man, age 14; OOG, a young
4   man, age 15; UGG, wife of OGG, age 11; IGG, age 23, chief
5   of the tribe; other MEN, WOMEN and CHILDREN of the
6   tribe.
7 **SETTING:** The action occurs in the Pleistocene era, many
8   thousands of years B.C. People have learned to live to-
9   gether as clans and tribes but have not yet developed a
10   verbal language. It is just after a long hunt. The entire
11   tribe sits around a big fire. They've all had a hard day of
12   hunting and being hunted. Everyone is dressed in animal
13   skins.
14   *(As the scene begins, all the characters sit staring into the*
15   *flames while dinner cooks on a spit.)*
16
17 **OGG:** *(Suddenly jumping to his feet)* **Ooo, uuh, ooo, uuh,**
18   **uhh.** *(OGG looks at the others, waiting for their reactions.*

1   *All of them turn to face OGG, puzzled looks on their ape-like*
2   *faces.)*
3   **OOG: Inga, inga inga. Uuk, uuk.** *(He taps a finger against*
4   *his temple and points to OGG as if to say: "You're crazy,*
5   *man. We don't behave like this in a social gathering.")*
6   **OGG:** *(Shaking his head in anger)* **Ooga, ooda, odda!**
7   **UGG:** *(Glancing from OGG to OOG)* **Poo, poo, poo, patowy.**
8   **IGG:** *(Spreading his hands, palms outward in a gesture indicat-*
9   *ing the others should be quiet)* **Sooda, sawda.** *(He nods*
10   *once and points toward OGG.)*
11   **OGG:** *(Baring his teeth in what must be a smile)* **Katuch,**
12   **katuch. Ick-ick.** *(Everyone now watches intently to see*
13   *what OGG will do. OGG walks inside the circle, just far*
14   *enough from the fire so his legs won't be scorched. He picks*
15   *up his bow, which had been lying beside his wife UGG. He*
16   *pulls an imaginary arrow from the skin quiver on his back,*
17   *crouches and sneaks around the entire circle. Then he mo-*
18   *tions to OOG and IGG to join him. They do, all crouching*
19   *now, slowly circling the fire. Suddenly OOG stops, the*
20   *others nearly bumping into him. He sights off into the dis-*
21   *tance, motions the others to follow. Suddenly, he raises his*
22   *bow, aims and shoots his imaginary arrow. OGG and IGG*
23   *do the same with the bows. Suddenly, they race around the*
24   *circle. UGG kneels, draws a sharp flint stone from his belt*
25   *and slices the neck of an imaginary animal. Then he and*
26   *the other two slit the imaginary belly, and pantomime drag-*
27   *ging the creature back to the campfire, all of them laughing,*
28   *slapping each other's backs and making strange verbal*
29   *sounds of excitement. Grins on their faces, they look at the*
30   *other tribe members, who are laughing and jabbering ex-*
31   *citedly.)*

In all probability, this is the way theatre began, as a reenact-
ment of something important in the lives of primitive people.
Later, instead of acting out the hunt after it happened, prehistoric
people began acting out what they wanted to happen in the next
day's hunt.

The acting became a kind of ritual, a way of making sure that the hunt would be successful.

Exercises

1. Think of what might have been other important events in the lives of prehistoric people. Just for fun, start acting out one of these things. As soon as your classmates understand what you are doing, invite two or three of them to continue the activity with you. You can use verbal sounds but not real words. Be as expressive as you can with these sounds.
2. Think of something in your own life that is important to you. Act it out for members of your class. Make it as exact as you can. See how quickly you can make them understand what you are portraying.

As language developed, people and their art both became more sophisticated. Art, including theatre, became more elaborate because people now could communicate with each other with much more exactness or precision.

As early as 3000 B.C. Egyptians began to record plays, although nobody knows whether or not these plays were performed. But the culture of Egypt was greatly admired by the citizens of ancient Greece. Most of our own theatre evolved from Greek theatre. This means that in all probability our theatre is based, in a second-hand sort of way, based on or derived from what the Egyptians did 5000 years ago.

The play or the written script is an important part of theatre. Except when actors are doing improvisations (making up the scenes as they go along), a script is the most important element of a theatrical production. Even in improvisation, there usually is an outline of some sort, although it often is very brief. This outline is the script.

Very simply, theatre is a play that is presented before an audience.

Exercises

1. Choose a two-character scene in a play and read it over several times but do not memorize the lines. Now, with a partner write a short outline of the scene and go over

it until you have it in mind. Using just the outline, present the scene with improvised dialog. Have someone tape what you do so you can see how you changed the lines.

2.   Now actually memorize the same scene and perform it for the class. Again, have someone tape the performance. Compare the two versions. Which do you like better? Why? Which do you think came across better? Why?

How Theatre Differs from Other Art Forms

Unlike some of the other art forms, theatre involves many people: actors, directors, stage carpenters, costume and make-up designers, producers, stage managers and more. A painting or a piece of sculpture usually involves only one artist.

Another difference is that plays use dialog or language to reach the audience. An overture, for instance, uses only music. A painting uses only colors and forms. Opera and other types of singing, of course, use words, but in a different way.

Theatre, like dance and opera, differs from many other art forms, in that it is "temporal." This means that unlike a piece of sculpture, it cannot be seen all at once because it exists in time. After it's presented, it's over and done with. It cannot be repeated again in exactly the same way. Different people collaborate on different productions of a play, and they all interpret it differently. Even the same production changes from one night to the next. Actors say their lines differently; the audience laughs in different places and so on.

All forms of art show how the artist looks at life. But because actors usually are trying to convince the audience that the action is really happening, theatre goes a lot further than many other art forms in imitating life, in allowing the audience to put themselves in the place of the characters.

Like all the other arts, theatre interprets life. Each of us sees things differently. One playwright will write about something in a different way than will any other playwright. Yet if playwrights are being honest—as they should be—they present life as they see it. Even so, their views may be a lot different from your view.

Theatre is different from many art forms because it's a combination of many arts. It uses architecture in the use of a setting, sculpture in the placement of furniture or other three-dimensional objects, a kind of dance in the planned movement of the actors, a kind of music in the dialog and painting in the set and make-up.

Theatre is like a kaleidoscope you turn in front of your eye. It is ever changing.

Exercises

1. Divide into groups of four or six. Find a two-character scene in a play. If you wish, it can be something from later chapters of the book. Choose a partner from within your group and go off by yourselves—maybe at lunch-time or after school—and rehearse the scene a few times. Then come back and present it to the class. Then see how different this is from the way the others in your group present the same scene. Discuss the differences and why you think they happened.

2. Choose another scene from a play. Try to figure out what the playwright is saying about life and how he or she views life. How do you view it differently? Why do you?

Reasons for Studying Theatre

Theatre is Fun

At least one of the reasons people like the theatre is because it is enjoyable. Theatre is a way of pretending and so escaping from the everyday routine of chores and homework. When we become involved in the production of a play, we enter a different world, a different universe. We escape into a make-believe existence where we can forget everyday cares.

Theatre takes us away from our problems and helps us to relax. It gives us the chance to create, which also makes us feel good. Some people like to create roles as characters in a play, others to create scenery and costumes. But whatever we create, if we do our best, we feel a sense of accomplishment, just as we do if we win a race or a ball game.

The playwright Berthold Brecht once said the theatre "needs no other passport than fun."

Theatre Builds Self-Confidence

When we learn how to design a set and then actually plan

the set for a play, we can tell ourselves: "Wow, that was fun, but I also learned to do something, and I learned to do it well."

The same is true for any facet of theatre. For instance, some people are much better than others at designing and hanging lights. If we are good at it, it gives us confidence that carries over to other parts of our lives. Maybe we wouldn't feel right about acting in front of a whole auditorium full of people. But then many actors wouldn't be able to light a show.

When we gain confidence in anything we do, this can carry over to the rest of our activities so that we approach them with more confidence as well.

Theatre Teaches Us About Life

Besides teaching us acting, directing and design, theatre can teach us important things about life. For instance, a play may be set in a foreign country. We may learn important things about the country itself and also about the way some people think. Fugard's *Master Harold and the Boys* takes place in South Africa, where the playwright lives. By seeing or working on his play, we learn about apartheid, racial discrimination, in which the government treated blacks and whites differently.

In plays like Fugard's, we learn about social issues. Later in the book there are scenes from two plays, *The Closing of the Mine* and *Going Steady*. In the first play a high school student is forced to face the fact that he not only is losing friends he's had all his life, but his family may very well lose their home. We learn to understand the boy and what it's like to confront important problems.

Going Steady is a less serious play. Nevertheless, it too takes a look at something important, the relationship between a boy and a girl who are at the age where they are beginning to become interested in the opposite sex.

The two plays teach us not only about particular problems but about people in general and how they are likely to react to many different situations.

This is another way of saying that a play should have both *universality* and *immediacy*.

Universality means that a work of art, in this case a play, has meaning for everyone in all places at all times. Of course, this is impossible since aboriginal tribes in Australia—or at least those members of the tribe who continue to live as their ancestors have lived for hundreds of years—will not be able to identify with or maybe even understand the actions of the characters in a play such as *The Odd Couple* (about two divorced men who live together). So maybe it's better to think of universality as a quality that affects the majority of people in different time periods.

Immediacy means that a play has meaning for people right now. A play that has universality will have immediacy because it has meaning for people in any age. But a play may have immediacy without universality.

An example of this latter type of play would be the rock musical, *Hair*, a big hit in the 1960s. It's not presented very often because it's outdated. For instance, it protested the military draft, which, of course, we don't even have anymore.

Theatre Teaches Appreciation

When you study theatre, you will learn to see what makes a production good or bad. Becoming acquainted with each part of theatre, you can see if the actors are performing as well as they should or if they aren't, and you'll be able to figure out why.

You'll know what makes a play good and why some plays are bad.

Knowing about the areas of design will help you judge what is good or bad. Most of all when you see a good production of a play, you'll have the background to understand and appreciate it.

This is just like anything else. If you understand the different moves a gymnast makes and have practiced gymnastics and can judge the difficulty of each movement, then you can appreciate better how a particular gymnast works. The same is true of the theatre. The more you know about it, the more you can appreciate it.

Exercises

1. Read a play and figure out what it taught you, if anything, that you didn't already know.
2. Discuss in class whether you felt the play had universality. Immediacy. Why?
3. Decide whether or not you think the play is a good one. What makes it good or bad? Do you think the playwright could have done better? Why? How could it be improved?

Theatre in Everyday Life

The Mimetic Instinct

We all learn through imitation or by what is often called the *mimetic instinct*. Infants learn to walk and talk by imitating others around them. If we are unsure how to act when we are at a party or eating unfamiliar food, we learn what to do by watching others. Put another way, this means we learn through example.

Theatre, of course, is carrying the mimetic instinct further. According to the ancient Greek philosopher Aristotle, the theatre "is an imitation of an action." That means playwrights observe human beings in a number of situations and learn how they are likely to behave. Then they take what they've learned, change it a little bit (or maybe a lot) and write a play.

You can understand this sort of thing by thinking of a basketball team. Most kids learn to shoot baskets by watching others. A coach then takes what he has learned—mostly by watching others and playing himself—and gives the members of the team pointers. Yet players like Michael Jordan or Magic Johnson improve upon what they learned. They take the basics further. This is what theatre does in imitating life.

Everyday Ritual

Primitive people established rituals in the form of pan-tomime and dances to assure enough rainfall for their crops. This sort of thing then is close to theatre, which actually developed from ritual and for a long time was associated with the church and religion.

We use ritual often in our everyday lives. There's a certain ritual or pattern to the school day and more of a ritual to religious services which usually follow a similar pattern each time. Some organizations have passwords and secret handshakes, which is a form of ritual. Sporting events follow a ritual, from the fans wearing the team colors to the playing of the national anthem to the introduction of the players.

This sort of thing is close to theatre. We rehearse and present a play, usually for more than one performance. The other rituals also are rehearsed by doing them over and over again, though they may vary more from one time to the next than theatre does. For example, the Christian church uses actors (the clergy) and the audience (the congregation) in the ritual of communion. Although we don't formally rehearse this sort of thing, we do learn by imitation how to act.

Young kids often play "house" or "cops and robbers." They are learning about life through imitation while at the same time they are assuming roles that are outside themselves.

In this kind of "play-acting" they are learning about life. This is exactly what we do as actors in a play.

Role Playing in Everyday Life

Every day we "become" many different people. We play the role of student for our teachers, friend for our friends, son or daughter for our parents. Adults in turn play the role of father or mother, cousin or aunt, as well as office worker or delivery person.

Depending on the situation, we act a certain way that does not fit other situations. For instance, you and your best friend are at your house. Now you are forced to play two roles, son or daughter and friend. This sometimes leads to whispering or asking to be excused from one set of "audience members" to act differently with the other.

There is nothing wrong with this, and we do not really become different people. We just show a different part of ourselves in each type of situation.

What roles are being played in this photo?

Exercises

1. Discuss the sort of things you have learned through imitation. What part does the mimetic instinct presently play in your life?
2. What rituals are now part of your life? Do you like them all? If you could, would you change or discard any of them? Why?
3. What sort of pretending do you see in everyday life? How do you feel about it? Discuss this with your class.
4. Try to figure out how many different roles you play each day. Have your teacher make a list on the chalkboard. Are there any roles you especially like or dislike? Why?
5. How many different roles do you see your mother or father playing in everyday life? Do you think that they especially like or dislike any of these roles? What makes you think so?

Opportunities for Theatre

There are many opportunities for you to become involved in theatre. Maybe it won't be with an elaborate production but, even so, you can get experience that can help you later.

Many schools have theatre, and this is a good place to begin to learn. Theatre in the schools exists mostly to teach. It gives experience to those involved in the production and provides entertainment and learning for the audience as well.

Since you are in a theatre class, this means your school has some sort of theatre program. Maybe you really want to be an actor. That's fine, but don't be disappointed or discouraged that you didn't get a role in a school production. Instead, work on helping to design or build the set or do make-up or properties. In this way you'll get an overall understanding of how theatre works.

Many religious groups present plays. Maybe you can get involved there. You may have a better chance than you would in school where there are probably more people your age who want to work on a production.

Don't overlook community theatre. Many plays have student-age characters or would be glad to have you lend a hand as part of the stage crew.

If you live close to a college, you might try to find out if there's a weekend or summer class for younger students. Many colleges have them. So do many community theatres. Sometimes summer stock theatres have classes for young people.

In some areas there are community cultural programs which include classes in theatre and the chance to be in a production. As a service of the Parks and Recreation Division, many cities have summer training programs for those interested in theatre.

If you live in a larger city that has professional theatres, you might take classes there or you might have the chance to be involved in actual productions. For instance, the Old Globe Theatre in San Diego has a training program for young actors, and like many other larger areas, San Diego has a special school for students interested in the performing arts.

There are opportunities in nearly any location to become involved in theatre if you want to.

Exercises

1.   Make a list of the types of theatre activity available in your community.

2.   Investigate one particular theatre (school, church, community or professional) and make a report to the class on how to become involved with it. Include the types of help you can give the theatre.

CHAPTER TWO
What Is Theatre?

From the beginning, theatre (like all forms of art) developed certain rules.

Theatrical Conventions

The rules of theatre are called "conventions." Many were first described by Aristotle in *The Poetics*. Aristotle (384 to 322 B.C.) was discussing tragedy, but the elements he described apply to theatre overall. Some, he said, are very important, others less so.

The Elements of Drama

By Aristotle's ranking, the elements from least to most important are *spectacle, melody, dialog, thought, character* and *plot*.

Spectacle is anything that affects how or what we see, such as the scenery or make-up.

The scenery has several purposes. It shows where the action occurs and provides either a background for the actors or an environment which partly surrounds them like the walls of a living room. Sometimes the scenery shows the historical period and the season of year. In Lee Blessing's *A Walk in the Woods*, for example, the action occurs outside where colored leaves continue to fall.

Through color, set dressings (like paintings) and properties (the furniture and the things the actors handle), the scenery can set a mood. This is the case with the spooky castle in *The Rocky Horror Picture Show*.

Setting, along with costuming, often helps tell what a character is like. If the setting is a shabby apartment and the clothes are out of style and worn, the audience will think that the characters don't have much money, or else they are eccentric. Sometimes a setting tells the audience what a character does. An example is the barber shop in *Sweeny Todd*.

Setting and properties show the tastes of the characters in the way the set is furnished. They can show the characters' interests and hobbies like in *You Can't Take it With You* where a set of barbells shows one of the characters is interested in body-building.

Make-up helps show what type of person the character is, and lighting can show time of day and help set the mood.

Melody is the rhythm of the language. For example, tragedy

has a slower rhythm than comedy. This is just like everyday life. When we are excited or having fun, we talk faster than when we are sad.

Dialog is closely related to the melody since we all speak differently depending on our mood. The dialog has to suit the characters.

Thought or intellect means the way the playwright develops ideas. A play should be the story of an individual but also should have a wide appeal.

Character is the main way the story unfolds. Unless it is intended to be silly or funny, a play shouldn't rely on fate or coincidence to solve characters' problems. Things can happen to the characters, but the important thing is how they react. A character also has to be an individual to be interesting but must have traits with which everyone can identify.

Plot is the action line and shows how the events unfold. The plot is what lets the writer bring the characters and ideas to an audience.

Exercises

1. Discuss why you think Aristotle said spectacle is the least important and plot the most important elements of drama.
2. Invent a setting that could tell a lot about the characters in a play. Tell the rest of the class what you have planned and see if they can figure out things about the characters.
3. Write a short scene in which two characters are angry with each other. Write another scene in which they are planning a trip to an amusement park. How is the way they talk affected by their moods?
4. Write another short scene in which a plumber and a chef are talking about their favorite hobbies. How will each one's way of talking differ from the others'? Why?
5. With someone else in class, use characters from Exercise 3 or 4 and write a short scene that introduces a problem one of the two characters has. In dialog and action, show how the problem is resolved.

Acting Conventions

Poet and writer Samuel Taylor Coleridge (1772-1834 and

probably best known for his poems *The Rhyme of the Ancient Mariner* and *Kubla Khan*) said that theatre should involve "a willing suspension of disbelief."

He meant that the audience has to be willing to enter into a world of "make-believe" and accept it as real. If the play is a good one and the characters are true to life, it isn't hard to suspend disbelief. As audience members, we want to become involved with the characters. Yet, if we stopped to think about it, we'd see that the production is not "real" at all.

In order to believe it is real, we have to accept many *theatrical conventions*, which are devices or "tools" for advancing the story.

Those involved in the production of a play try to create an *illusion of reality*, which most often we are willing to accept in the same way we "accept" that a magician's tricks are real. Even though we actually know they aren't real and neither is a play, we push aside this knowledge and enter into the world the magician or theatre artists have created.

Here is a list of some acting conventions, several still in use, others now outdated except for parodies.

1. The proscenium arch. This divides the stage from the audience and provides a frame around the action. Usually, the audience is supposed to pretend they can see through an imaginary fourth wall.

2. Voice projection. The actors on stage, particularly if the auditorium is big, speak more loudly than they would in a real-life situation.

3. Actor placement. Unless there is a good reason for it, actors rarely turn their backs on the audience. In most cases the actors move in front of the furniture instead of behind it, and they make sure they can be easily seen from all areas in the auditorium.

4. Gestures. Actors, especially in a theatre, make broader gestures than people in everyday life do. This is so the audience can more easily see them. (See photo on page 18.)

Exercises

1. As a class, make a list of any other acting conventions you can think of.
2. Discuss why you think an audience is willing to accept theatrical conventions.

This photo illustrates the use of broad gestures.

Writing Conventions

Playwrights use a variety of conventions. Most are used in order for the playwright to be selective. That is they eliminate anything that isn't important to the plot, and they also are a kind of shorthand. For example, in old-fashioned melodramas, it's easy to pick out the villain because of his dark suit and curling moustache. Here are some of the conventions playwrights use:

1. The soliloquy. Rarely used anymore, the soliloquy is a device in which a character reveals innermost thoughts by saying them aloud, just as we often talk to ourselves when we are alone. The purpose is to show the character's feelings in an abbreviated manner. Probably the best known soliloquy is Hamlet's which begins, "To be, or not to be . . ."

2. The aside. Also not used much anymore, this is a speech delivered directly to the audience by one of the characters and was popular in exaggerated melodramas. Supposedly, the other characters are unable to hear what

is said. Often during an aside the other characters "freeze" while the villain tells the audience how he plans to kidnap the heroine and take all her money.

3. The monolog. This is a long speech delivered by a character in a play, usually to the audience, but sometimes to other characters. If you ever saw *Our Town*, you know the Stage Manager (a character in the play) speaks to the audience when he talks about Grover's Corners, New Hampshire.

4. The flashback. The audience sees a scene that occurred before the time in which the play exists. The audience usually is asked to believe they can see into a character's mind while the person is remembering something from the past. In Miller's *Death of a Salesman*, for instance, Willy remembers when his sons were boys, and the audience "sees" his thoughts.

5. Exposition. This is any background information the audience needs to understand the play. The soliloquy, the aside, the monolog and the flashback all are ways of filling in background details. Exposition also can be presented through setting, lighting, make-up and costuming to show the sort of place in which the characters live, the season of the year, the sort of people the characters are and so on.

6. Dramatic time. Events usually progress faster on the stage than in real life. The characters express themselves more clearly and more concisely than people generally do. They leave out unnecessary details, which are ordinarily part of real-life conversations. The audience is asked to accept that an hour of playing time may represent almost any amount of time—from an actual hour to many years.

7. The framework. This refers to the "universe" in which a play takes place. The framework may be very similar to what we know in real life, or it may be something completely different. For instance, in children's theatre, animals often talk and act like human beings. In science fiction plays, the audience often is asked to imagine they are on another planet.

Exercises

1. With one of your classmates come up with a short scene

you can perform together in which you use either a monolog delivered to the audience, or an aside.

2. Write a set description and the first page of a script that creates a universe that is much different from our own. This could be for a historical play, a place where magic is practiced, a play that occurs years into the future and so on.

Production Conventions

There are many conventions that are part of the physical production.

1. Setting. This is the environment or background for the play and, of course, is a representation of a locale. Sometimes the setting is very realistic; sometimes it just suggests a location. If the action takes place inside a living room, for instance, it is usually much larger than most real living rooms. Also in a real house, the furniture is usually closer together and is arranged differently, usually along four walls instead of three. The walls in a real house are not angled outward as they are in most stage settings.
2. Flats. These are frames constructed of one-by-three boards and covered with canvas which is then painted. Most often flats are used to suggest walls of a building.
3. Properties. Often called props, hand properties are objects used or handled by actors. Often they are not "practical," that is, they are not really what they represent. A gun does not have real bullets but blanks. A letter may really be a blank piece of paper and so on. Set properties are the furnishings.
4. Stage lighting. This is artificial lighting and not sunlight or moonlight. Stage lighting also eliminates many of the shadows we would see in everyday life. The lights on stage are usually brighter than those in a real house.
5. Make-up. Most often the make-up on the stage is much heavier than that in real life. It often suggests differences in the way a person looks, like giving the character a bigger nose, different colored hair, scars and so on.

Genre

Another kind of theatrical convention is genre, which means

the way a play is classified, and how the playwright treats the subject matter.

There are two main ways of treating subject matter, serious and comic.

Tragedy

The "heaviest" or most serious genre is tragedy. The playwright tries to have the audience identify completely with the protagonist who always struggles against overwhelming odds and so is defeated.

Tragedy deals with profound problems. Even when tragic characters die, their heroism lives.

Comedy

The opposite of tragedy is comedy. Often the playwright wants us to laugh at ourselves and our customs so that we'll take them less seriously. We don't usually identify with a comic protagonist so much as with a tragic one.

Unlike tragedy, comedy ends happily. If the protagonist were defeated, the audience would feel guilty for laughing.

There are certain devices a playwright can use to make a play funny. They are derision, incongruity, exaggeration, repetition, surprise and character inconsistency.

Derision means poking fun at people or customs.

Incongruity means placing opposites together. An example would be a man wearing a tuxedo coat and torn jeans.

Exaggeration means making things bigger or overstating them. For example, people are not as greedy or nasty as Cinderella's stepmother and stepsisters are in the Stephen Sondheim musical, *Into the Woods*.

Repetition means using a verbal or visual gag over and over. An example would be a man's tripping over a doormat each time he enters or leaves a house.

Surprise simply is the unexpected. We know every joke will have a punch line, but we don't know what it will be.

Character inconsistency means a personality trait that does not seem to fit with the others. In *Arsenic and Old Lace* the two aunts are sweet old ladies except that they murder old men.

Melodrama

Melodrama combines elements of comedy and tragedy. It

deals with a serious subject but has a happy ending. Unlike tragic characters, those in melodrama are often one-dimensional rather than being well-rounded.

Melodrama often relies on coincidence or fate to intensify and then help solve the protagonist's problem. Good always triumphs.

Farce

Farce is similar to melodrama in that fate plays a part in the outcome. But it is more closely related to comedy because it exists just for fun. It uses "stock" characters—those that are only types and have no depth. The plots, which are not at all believable, rely on a lot of physical actions, sly behavior and twists and turns in the action. The plot, which relies on misunderstandings, shows how the major characters manage to get themselves out of situations in which they've become entangled.

Tragicomedy

In tragicomedy a situation often appears comic, but later the audience realizes it's serious. This is because tragicomedy tries to show that life itself is a mixture of the comic and the tragic.

Style

There are two basic styles. One is "representation," the other "presentation." The playwright who uses representation wants the audience to accept that what they are viewing is life.

The playwright who uses presentation is not trying to convince the audience that the play is "real." In this sort of play, the audience is reminded over and over that they are not seeing "life," but rather something that talks about life.

Most serious plays are "representational," lighter plays, "presentational." Many plays mix the two styles. When the Stage Manager in *Our Town* talks to the audience, that is presentational. But there are other scenes when the characters do not acknowledge the audience at all.

Naturalism and realism are representational styles. Naturalism means putting everything on stage that would be found in life. Realism means using only what is necessary to create the illusion of life.

Expressionism and symbolism are presentational styles.

Expressionism, in writing and design, shows the protagonist's inner self and how he or she views the world. Symbolism uses one thing to stand for another. Platforms or undefined shapes can stand for rocks or trees.

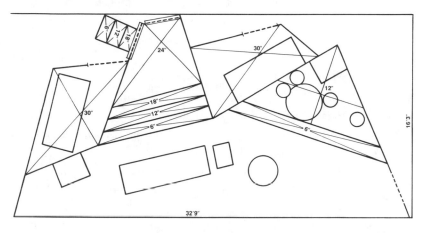

In the floor plan for this expressionistic set the living room stretches across the stage because the central character likes to entertain. The kitchen is odd-shaped (a triangle) because she tries to push everyday routine into a corner. The two bedrooms, her kids' rooms, are odd-shaped because she looks upon her kids as things that have twisted her life out of shape.

Exercises

1. Following are scenes from three plays. The first is a tragedy, the second a comedy, the third a melodrama. With the rest of the class, figure out and discuss why each fits its category. *(Exercises are continued on page 29)*

A Thing of Beauty
by Charles Kray

1
2
3
4 ***CHARACTERS:*** PRIORESS, COLONEL, BENE-
5 DICTA.
6 ***SETTING:*** The scene is the receiving room of a convent
7 in Germany. The time is the late 1930s. It is dusk.
8 An elderly nun, the PRIORESS of the convent, is

1	pacing around the room. There is a knock at the door
2	and she hurries to open it. A Nazi COLONEL enters.
3	He is about forty. The PRIORESS is visibly agitated
4	and through the ensuing formalities is impatient.
5	The COLONEL is ill at ease in her presence.
6	
7	PRIORESS: Come in, Eric.
8	COLONEL: Thank you, Reverend Mother.
9	PRIORESS: Please sit down.
10	COLONEL: Thank you. *(She sits and he does also.)*
11	It's been a long time, Sister.
12	PRIORESS: Yes, time passes much too quickly.
13	COLONEL: You haven't changed much.
14	PRIORESS: You have. I've read about you.
15	COLONEL: *(Ignores the remark but his manner becomes*
16	*harder.)* What can I do for you, madam?
17	PRIORESS: I received news of my sisters.
18	COLONEL: I expected you would.
19	PRIORESS: Is it true then?
20	COLONEL: I'm afraid so.
21	PRIORESS: But why?
22	COLONEL: We both know why, Sister.
23	PRIORESS: No, I don't. I don't understand why
24	nineteen innocent nuns are taken off a train like
25	criminals and sent to a concentration camp. We
26	are Germans. We have done nothing to be
27	treated this way.
28	COLONEL: Sister, you have been warned, as every
29	Carmelite convent in this area, that we mean to
30	have Edith Stein. If you are Germans, then give
31	her up to us.
32	PRIORESS: There is no Edith Stein here.
33	COLONEL: Perhaps not. But we know that she is
34	in Germany, hiding in a Carmelite convent. Your
35	nuns are being held as hostage. If we do not

1 apprehend Edith Stein, the nuns will suffer the
2 consequences. Nineteen for one.
3 PRIORESS: Why is she so important?
4 COLONEL: She is a Jew.
5 PRIORESS: Is this a crime to be a Jew?
6 COLONEL: It will be.
7
8
9 # We Are, You Are, They Are
10
11 *CHARACTERS:* JIM, DOTTY, BILL, SALLY, PRO-
12 FESSOR, JUNE.
13 *SETTING:* The action occurs in a classroom of one of
14 the largest universities in the Western Hemisphere.
15 There is a teacher's desk Right, in front of which are
16 two rows of six student desks, three desks to a row.
17 A doorway is in the Upper Right Corner.
18 *(As the play opens, JIM is standing Center, facing*
19 *the audience. He is a typical college student in typical*
20 *college dress. DOTTY is seated at one of the front row*
21 *desks nearest the audience. Her appearance suggests*
22 *that she is an intellectual.)*
23
24 JIM: I go to this university. It's a large university.
25 One of the largest universities in the Western
26 Hemisphere.
27 DOTTY: I have found that according to Sir Walter
28 Raleigh's *History of the World* sodium chloride
29 and a Greek periaktoi, when mixed together
30 with a diminished seventh, result in a stream-of-
31 consciousness technique similar to that em-
32 ployed by the late William Faulkner in his
33 triolets of Admiral Byrd at the Equator. There-
34 fore, the tendency is to I sing, you sing, he, she,
35 it sings. We sing, you sing, they shall have done

1   been singed.

2   **JIM:** *(Still addressing the audience)* **Dotty is very**

3   **studious. She's only eighteen, and next month**

4   **she will assume the post of intellectual overseer**

5   **at Harvard Girls' School.**

6   **DOTTY:** *(To the audience)* **The professor will soon be**

7   **here. That is to say he shortly will arrive.**

8   **JIM:** *(Turning toward DOTTY)* **How astute.**

9   **DOTTY:** *(To JIM)* **I've prepared my assignment. I'll**

10   **receive an A-plus.**

11   **JIM:** *(Again to the audience)* **This class is small. There**

12   **are just two other members of the class.** *(He sits*

13   *beside DOTTY at a desk on which are lying his*

14   *textbook and notebook. BILL enters. He is the clean-*

15   *cut, all-American-boy type. He carries a loose-leaf*

16   *folder and several books.)*

17   **BILL:** *(Taking a few steps into the classroom)* **Good af-**

18   **ternoon, fellow students. I'm a clean-cut, all-**

19   **American boy. I've come to class because, as**

20   **you know, I'm from one of the most touted**

21   **minority groups in the United States today. In**

22   **other words, I am Protestant, white and twenty-**

23   **one. I also run the hundred-yard dash in 7.9 sec-**

24   **onds. Or is it in 9.7? Oh, well, it doesn't matter.**

25   **What does matter is that I impress you, my fel-**

26   **low classmates, and the good professor doctor**

27   **that my ethnic, religious and national back-**

28   **ground is just as good as yours. Therefore I try**

29   **to be punctual.** *(He sits at one of the desks behind*

30   *and Downstage of JIM and DOTTY.)*

31

32

33   # Each Man in His Time

34

35   ***CHARACTERS:*** LARRY, 35, an M.D. and medical

1 researcher at UCSD; WILL, a very confused man.

2 **SETTING:** The action occurs in an upper-class con-

3 dominium in La Jolla, a wealthy section of San Diego.

4 *(This scene occurs about two-thirds of the way into*

5 *the play. LARRY wears a rumpled suit and thick*

6 *glasses. WILL wears a beige linen shirt with puffed*

7 *sleeves, velvet pants and moccasin-like boots. He is*

8 *bald except for a fringe of grey hair. He has a wispy*

9 *moustache.)*

10

11 **LARRY:** *(Seated on a plush looking sofa Stage Right)*

12 **In short, Bill, by applying the latest develop-**

13 **ments in a dozen fields of science, we found we**

14 **could revitalize a cell long after death, by what-**

15 **ever definition you'd want to use. But it had to**

16 **be a special cell. One that didn't break down**

17 **easily. In other words, a bone cell.**

18 **WILL: But tell why thy canonized bones, hearsed**

19 **in death, have burst their cerements; why the**

20 **sepulchre, wherein we saw them quietly**

21 **inurn'd, hath oped his ponderous and marble**

22 **jaws, to cast thee up again.**

23 **LARRY: An apt analogy, I suppose. But there were**

24 **many unknowns. Would the new organism be**

25 **like the parent in every respect? Or wouldn't it?**

26 **Theoretically, any cell of a living entity contains**

27 **the imprint of the entire being. And so any cell**

28 **can be cloned and become, in effect, a duplicate**

29 **of the original.** *(Pause)* **At the university we're**

30 **still experimenting with rats.**

31 **WILL: Yes?**

32 **LARRY:** *(Rising and gazing out the Upstage window)* **I**

33 **have this passion, you see. For theatre . . . and**

34 **plays. And for me one playwright stands out above**

35 **all the others. His name is William Shakespeare.**

1 WILL: What does all this have to do with me?
2 LARRY: You don't have much experience in know-
3   ing other people. But surely you've noticed we
4   live well. *(WILL nods.)* Money buys a lot of things.
5   Things the average person probably doesn't
6   even suspect. *(Chuckling)* I could indulge my
7   passion a little more than most. I wanted some
8   cells and I got them. *(He turns to WILL.)* It isn't
9   very noble of me, but I bribed a few people.
10   *(Walks to the sofa and sits.)* Of course, I took a
11   chance. Shakespeare lived so long ago that there
12   were many unknowns. All I took was a micro-
13   scopic sample. Then when I returned to the
14   States, I rented warehouse space and set up my
15   own lab. *(Pause)* There could be all sorts of legal
16   implications . . . when you try to clone a person.
17 WILL: What person did you— Oh, dear God!
18 LARRY: I see you understand.
19 WILL: When we are born, we cry that we are come
20   to this great stage of fofools! *(He sobs.)* Why? Why?
21   Thou know'st, the first time that we smell the
22   air we wawl and cry. And yet, a second time you
23   bring me forth!
24 LARRY: Yes, and now you have a chance to live
25   again. To use that great mind of yours to its
26   fullest potential. You were barely into your
27   fifties. You were cheated; the world was cheated.
28 WILL: You had no right.
29 LARRY: I had every right. Oh, maybe not legally.
30   And some people would say not morally. But—
31 WILL: What am I?
32 LARRY: You are William Shakespeare, one of the
33   greatest poets who ever lived.
34 WILL: I'm a fragment. *(He screams in rage and frus-*
35   *tration.)*

(Exercises continued from page 23.)

2. What style of design would work for each of the three scenes? What makes you think so?
3. Write a page of dialog that fits into the category of comedy, tragedy, melodrama, farce or tragicomedy. Read it to your class and see if they can figure out which it is and why they think so.

CHAPTER THREE
Theatres and Stages

Theatre Structures

There are three main types of theatre structures.

The Proscenium Theatre

The most common type of theatre has a proscenium stage, often called a picture frame stage because it has an arch that frames the acting area. The audience faces the stage and for most plays is expected to believe that they are viewing the action through an imaginary fourth wall.

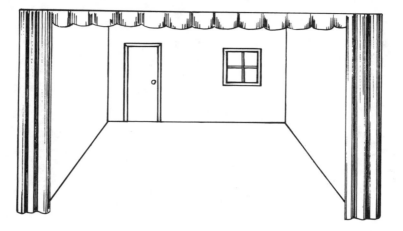

In a theatre with a proscenium stage, the audience is physically separated from the actors and, before the play starts and between acts, the stage can be closed off with a front curtain, called a *grand drape.*

The settings can be more realistic than on any other type of stage, so this is the easiest type of theatre in which to produce representational plays. In a majority of plays the action occurs inside a house or apartment. This allows the set designer to use flats. Remember that these are frames covered with canvas. They can be placed side-by-side to look like walls. (They also can be constructed with windows and doors.) This effect is called a *box set* because it resembles a box, except that usually the walls are angled out from back to front to allow those in any part of the

auditorium to have a good view of the action.
If a box set were arranged like this:

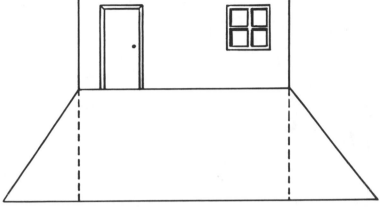

those sitting on the far right and the far left wouldn't be able to see inside all of the box.

A box set provides an "environment" in which the actors can perform, rather than having them act in front of it. This is another reason the production can appear true to life.

Other types of scenery also can be used in a proscenium theatre. One kind is the *backdrop*, sometimes just called a *drop*. This also uses theatrical canvas, but instead of attaching it to a frame, the canvas hangs from rods called *battens* and is weighted at the bottom. The backdrop is painted, either to represent indoor or outdoor scenes, and usually stretches the length of the stage.

Along with drops, curtains are used to mask the backstage area and the *fly space*, the area directly behind the top of the arch and above the floor of the stage. There are two types of curtains, *teasers* and *tormenters*. Teasers are short curtains that stretch the length of the stage and mask the fly space where the lighting instruments are hung. Tormenters are longer curtains, stretching from the battens to the floor. They mask the backstage area.

An easy way to remember which type of curtain is which is to remember that the shorter curtain, teaser, also is the shorter word with only six letters, while the tormenter, the longer curtain, is a longer word since it has ten letters. Remember that the front curtain is called the grand drape and also extends to the floor. Tormenters can be the same sort of curtain but are always behind the grand drape.

All this may seem confusing, but the following will help you see how each of these appears.

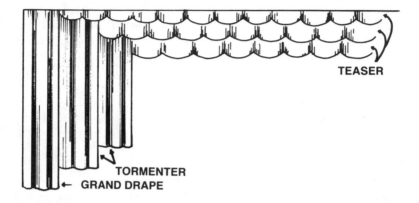

TEASER

TORMENTER

← **GRAND DRAPE**

Another piece of scenery that most often appears with backdrops is a *wing*. This may be confusing because the backstage areas, that is the areas on either side of the set, are also called the wings.

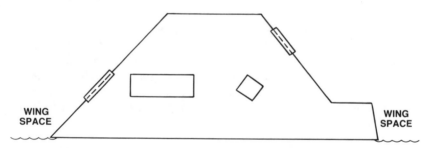

WING SPACE

WING SPACE

The scenery that is called a wing (because it extends into the wings), is really a flat that stands by itself and not as part of a box set. Usually wings are placed a short distance apart from the front to the back of a stage and, like teasers, mask the backstage area.

Often wings and backdrops are used together, and can be painted to suggest specific locations, though they don't appear to be as realistic as the box set. Many times *wing and drop* scenery is used just to suggest locations. In this case audiences are asked to imagine the "real" place.

Sometimes the wings are painted a neutral color so they can represent a variety of locations, while the backdrops suggest more specific scenes. This is because the drops can "be flown." This means they can be taken up as well as lowered from the fly space, which in many theatres is at least twice as high as the proscenium arch. This is especially helpful in plays, such as musicals, where there are many changes of scenery. It is quick and easy—a matter of a few seconds—to raise one backdrop and lower another using a system of ropes and pulleys called the *counterweight system*. A backdrop really is a background for the action rather than an environment. This means the actors perform in front of the scenery, rather than being in the middle of it like they are in a box set. Wing and drop scenery or drops used with tormenters are more "presentational," less realistic. Below is an example of a wing and drop set.

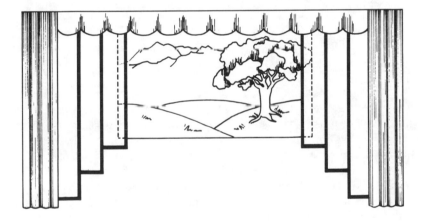

Scrims are semitransparent cloths, which usually are painted. These are a special kind of backdrop. When they are lighted from the front, they appear opaque or solid, and the audience sees a painted surface. When they are lighted from the back, the audience sees through them. The backlighting creates a dream-like effect.

Other two-dimensional scenery, such as cutouts, are sometimes used. They can be objects such as trees or hedges, and usually are cut out of ¼-inch plywood.

For outdoor scenes, particularly to give the effect of great distance, another piece of scenery is used. This is called a *cyclorama*, which is a circular curtain surrounding the sides and rear of the acting area, as shown below.

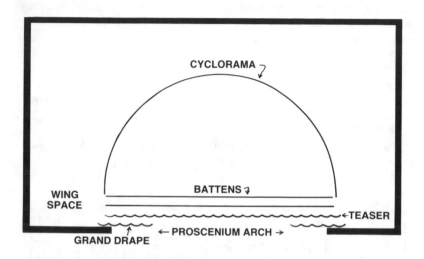

Sometimes a *wagon stage* is used in proscenium theatre. This is a platform that can be rolled on and off stage. It either fits into grooves in the stage floor or is built on casters.

The wagon stage can be either large or small, filling part of the stage or all of it. Like the backdrop, it is used for quick scenery changes. The disadvantage is that it requires a large backstage area where it can be stored when not in use.

Sometimes platforms are built on-stage to represent any number of things, a landing, a second story, rocks and so on. At other times the platforms represent unspecified locations.

When proscenium theatres were first used, during the Renaissance era, the stages were *raked* or sloped gradually upward from the front to the rear wall. Today's stages usually have a flat floor, though occasionally there are theatres still in use with raked stages.

Even if this type of theatre is no longer widely used, terms that originated with a raked stage have carried over to the present time. That is why *upstage* means the area furthest from the audience, while that closest to the audience is *downstage*.

Stage Right is the area to the actors' right as they face the audience, and *Stage Left* then is the actor's left facing the audience. *Center Stage*, of course is the center of the stage floor. *Up Center* is the middle area toward the back and *Down Center* is the center

This is the set for The Lion in Winter, *presented at Heidelberg College in Tiffin, Ohio. The platforms represent various rooms in a castle. (Photo by Jeff McIntosh.)*

of the stage closest to the audience. From this it is easy to figure out the other areas *Down Right* or *Left Center*. Usually in a script the names are abbreviated, such as *DL* (Down Left) or *UR* (Up Right).

The following drawing shows the areas of the stage.

UR UP RIGHT	UC UP CENTER	UL UP LEFT
RC RIGHT CENTER	C CENTER	LC LEFT CENTER
DR DOWN RIGHT	DC DOWN CENTER	DL DOWN LEFT

Most stages have at least a little bit of space in front of the proscenium arch. This area is called both the *apron* and the *forestage*. The further out it comes, the bigger the playing area. Aprons are often used for presentational plays.

There are several advantages to a proscenium stage. As you learned, the scenery can be more realistic, and the curtain can be closed for scenery shifts. Besides that actors can wait just off-stage for their cues, and scenery and props can be stored close to the acting area but away from the audience's view.

A disadvantage is that there cannot be the closeness between audience and actor that is desirable for some plays, particularly those done in a presentational style.

Exercises

1. Taking into consideration all you know about a proscenium theatre, read one of the plays in the book and figure out the kind of set that would work for it. Draw pictures of the set, looking down from above, for example:

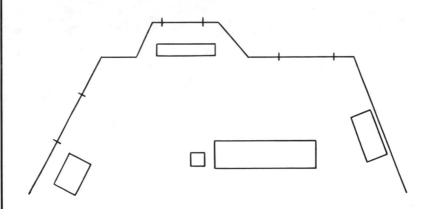

Then draw a picture of the set looking at it from the front: (See page 37 for example.)

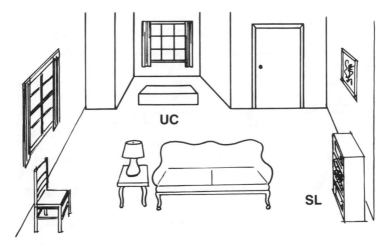

UC = Upstage Center   SL – Stage Left

2. Explain your setting to the rest of the class. Now choose a cast for a scene from the play and use an area of the classroom as your stage. Have the actors pretend the set already is in place. Now direct them as to where they should stand and where they should move.
3. If you designed a box set for your play, design another set that uses the wing and drop system or else uses tormenters and drops.

The Arena Theatre

In arena theatre, the audience surrounds the action. Despite this type of theatre often being called *theatre-in-the-round*, the acting area usually is square or oval. In proscenium theatre the stage usually is raised above the audience, but in arena theatre it usually is lower than the audience area The seats are raked downward from the outer walls of the theatre toward the stage.

Since the audience surrounds the action, realistic sets can't be used. Sometimes scrims are used with backlights but, usually, all the walls are imaginary.

Even though scenery is less realistic or even nonexistent, properties have to be more realistic for representational plays because the audience usually is closer to the action and can easily detect any poor substitutes.

In arena theatre, the terms for stage areas that are used for

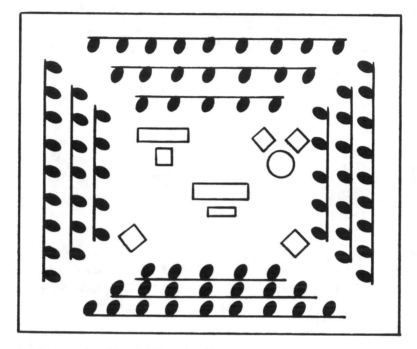

This is a bird's-eye view of an arena stage.

proscenium theatre have no meaning. Upstage for one part of the audience is downstage for another. So the acting area generally is divided like the time on a clock. One particular area, for instance, is established as twelve o'clock, and remains the same. Then other areas become the one o'clock position, the two o'clock position and on around the dial of a clock.

Sometimes the areas are designated by direction, for example, north, north east, east, south east and so on.

An advantage of arena theatre is the physical closeness between spectator and actor. Even though there cannot be an elaborate set, the audience still can feel more a part of the action. They can more easily see actors' facial expressions and subtle movement than they can from several rows back in a proscenium theatre.

Another advantage is that almost any space can be used since the playing area can be smaller than that of a proscenium stage. The seating area also covers a smaller space.

The major disadvantage is that it is difficult to conceal anything. There is a grid, an area of interconnection of pipes on which

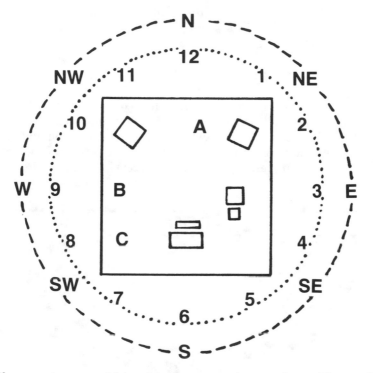

Shown are two ways of determining stage areas in arena theatre. They can be labeled by directions (the outside letters) or by the numbers on the dial of a clock.

lighting instruments are hung. Since these are directly above the stage area, the lights are in plain view of the audience.

Furniture and properties not in use either have to be stored in sight of the audience or have to be carried through the aisleways to the acting area. Actors cannot wait off-stage but usually have to make longer entrances and exits, where they come down the aisleways of the audience area.

Exercises

1. Furniture in an arena setting can be placed more like it really is in the room of a house, except that there probably will be more open space in the center of the room. With the same play you used for the proscenium stage, design a set for arena theatre.

2. Again, cast classmates to fill the roles in the play, and direct them in a scene, dividing the playing area like a clock or using directions.

The Thrust Stage

A third type of theatre is one that contains a thrust stage with a playing area similar to that of the arena theatre, except that one side opens into a stagehouse or back wall. The audience sits around the three remaining sides. Most often this kind of stage is lower than the audience, though occasionally it is higher.

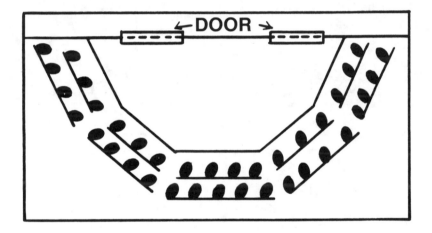

An example of a thrust stage.

Acting areas here can be called by the upstage/downstage names or by the north/south or clock positions of arena theatre.

Since there is a back wall, more scenery can be used than in arena theatre but not as much as on a proscenium stage. Box sets can't be used, but at least there can be a background for the actors. As in arena theatre, the audience is closer to the actor, and there is no physical separation such as there is in a proscenium theatre.

There are other kinds of stages, but they are really just variations of these three. Also, a great deal of difference exists among theatres of any particular type. Some proscenium theatres seat 50 or 100 spectators while others seat a thousand or more. Of course, intimate plays like the musical *The Fantasticks* would be less effective in a large theatre, and elaborate productions, such as the musical *Cats*, could not be presented easily in a theatre that seats less than 100.

Exercises

1. Again use the same play and design a set. Remember that you can use scenery as a background, but it may be hard for the audience on the extreme sides to see it. Now direct your actors in a scene.
2. Which type theatre structure do you prefer? Why? Which would you rather use as an actor, director, or designer? Which would you rather attend? Discuss this with the rest of the class.

CHAPTER FOUR
Writing a Play

The playwright is the first person to work on the production of a play. Since playwrights most often work alone, particularly in the beginning, they have more freedom to do as they please than do other theatre artists who must collaborate with everyone else.

Building Characters

Usually, character and plot are the two most important parts of a play. Think of any plays or movies you have seen, and you probably think first of the characters and then what happened to them.

Because of this, playwrights often begin with a character. How do they go about coming up with a person who is interesting and memorable? There are a lot of different ways.

Most important, they need to know the characters, which isn't as hard as it sounds.

The Character Interview

What would you do, for instance, if the editor of the school paper asked you to write an article about someone you don't know? How would you go about it? Of course, you would interview the person.

You can do the same thing with the characters for a play. There is an acting exercise called the "character interview." There are three rules:

1. You are not allowed to plan anything out ahead of time.
2. You cannot answer as yourself but as a character who is beginning to take shape.
3. All the answers have to be consistent, that is, they all should help make up a believable character.

In the acting version of this exercise a person agrees to be "it," and other people in class ask the person questions. For instance:

Q: What's your name?
A: Millie Brown.
Q: How old are you?
A: Seventy-two.

Q:	Where do you live?
A:	On earth's second moon.
Q:	What! I didn't know earth had a second moon.
A:	Oh, yes, but it's very small.
Q:	How did you get there?
A:	I was born there.
Q:	Does your family live there too?
A:	Yes, my mom and dad and my grandparents.
Q:	Your mom and dad and your grandparents? But you said you're seventy-two.
A:	Our days go by a lot faster than yours. I suppose in earth time I'd be fourteen or fifteen.
Q:	How did your family get to the moon?
A:	How did your family get on earth? I mean, we've lived there for years and years.
Q:	What do you do there?
A:	I go to school. I'm in grade fifty-two.
Q:	Fifty-two?
A:	I told you, our years are a lot shorter.
Q:	Listen, are you a human being?
A:	I'm a toad.
Q:	What?!
A:	Don't be silly. Of course, I'm a human being. I'm just different from you.
Q:	Oh? How are you different?
A:	Just look at me. Six arms, four legs, two eyes on my face and one on the back of my head.

As you see, there may be some surprises, but the character is consistent. Nothing really is contradictory.

The interesting thing is that you don't need to do this as an acting exercise. You can do it by yourself, playing both roles. Just let the questions and answers flow. If you want to, you can tape what happens. (Of course, the interview doesn't have to be as silly as the example. Usually, you'd probably want to develop more earthly-type characters.)

The character that begins to develop often can suggest situations or action.

Although you can do the exercise by yourself, it might be fun to try it with the rest of the class. Each person can spend two or three minutes being "it," with the rest of the class asking questions.

Word Association

Another way to develop characters is to use word association. This means beginning with any word and then saying the first thing that comes into your head. For example, suppose your first word is "cat." That might make you think of "dog," followed by "pets," "fleas," "flea collars," and so on.

When you use this to build a character, you start with a physical or personality trait, such as "handsome." Then say any other traits that grow out of this one: blue eyes, blond hair, boy, 16, shy, no self-confidence, smart.

After you have listed 10 or 12 traits, take four or five of them and start to develop a character by writing a "thumbnail sketch" of the person. Add whatever you like:

Tom Byronson is handsome. He has blond hair, blue eyes and a winning smile. The problem is that he is very shy and seems to have no self-confidence.

You can place the person in a setting:

When Tom Byronson first came to Central High School, nobody liked him. They thought he was stuck-up because he almost never talked. It took a long time for anyone to realize that he just didn't have any self-confidence, which was hard to believe in anyone so good-looking.

Maybe the character will suggest a story (a plot for your play) immediately:

Tom Byronson dreaded changing high schools. It had always been hard for him to make friends. But now that he had made them, he didn't want to have to start all over again.

He sat at the dining-room table with his mom and dad and his sister, Debbie, when all at once Dad announced the company was transferring him to the other end of the state.

It doesn't matter how you begin the character sketch. All that matters is that a believable person begins to emerge.

Learning to Know Your Character

What kinds of things should you know about your characters before you begin to write your play? They can be divided into five categories: 1) physical characteristics; 2) background; 3) attitudes and beliefs; 4) patterns of behavior; 5) dominant traits.

Physical characteristics includes things like height, weight, eye color, hair color and style. Background means the areas where the person grew up or lived, the type and amount of schooling, jobs and family life. Attitudes and beliefs include religion, politics, feelings for others, and interests. Patterns of behavior include how the person likes to spend spare time, what he or she does from day to day. Dominant traits mean the most important character traits, such as stinginess, helpfulness and so on.

Of course, all these things are related. For instance, a person's educational and family background affect attitudes and behavior.

It's a good idea to figure out as much about the character as you can. That way you can make the person believable for an audience.

Maybe some of the character's traits suggest locations and situations, such as Tom Byronson having to transfer to a new school. You have two settings, home and school. It also suggests a conflict which is the beginning of a plot: He does not want to go to the new school because he fears trying to make new friends.

Exercises

1. Develop two characters through word association. Maybe one will suggest the other, like Tom's character suggested those of his parents. Then include the two characters in a one-minute scene that you write.
2. Figure out what traits you most like in a friend. Develop a character based on these traits. Do the same thing with traits that you dislike. Now put the two characters who came from this into a one-minute scene that you write.
3. Figure out the most important traits of two fictional characters, such as Captain Picard on *Star Trek: The Next Generation*, and Pinocchio. Give one of Picard's traits to Pinocchio and one of Pinocchio's to Picard. Think of a place they might meet and what they might say to each other. Write a two-minute scene based on this.
4. Write a one-page character sketch of the most interesting person you saw today. What makes the person particularly interesting?

Just as it is impossible to get to know a person in real life in just a few hours, so too an audience cannot begin to know nearly everything about a character in a few hours of playing time. So as a playwright, even though you know as much about your characters as possible, you just do not have the time to include all of these things in a play. You have to decide what is most important to know about the person to communicate whatever is important to the play's central idea. You have to decide what you want to say to an audience.

For instance, if you're in a certain situation and are trying to do something—pass a test maybe or win a sporting event—you don't reveal a great amount about yourself while doing these two things. So a character in a play cannot reveal all sorts of things about himself or herself when trying to reach one particular goal.

Conflict and Action

Characters are what usually grab an audience's interest, but the plot, which is made up of conflict and action, is what continues to hold this interest. The plot tells a story. It tells how the main character, called the protagonist, meets opposition and deals with it.

The person or thing that opposes the protagonist is the antagonist, who tries to stop the main character from getting something he or she wants or needs.

The action begins when the protagonist and antagonist first clash and ends either when the central character is able to reach his or her goal or else fails.

Sometimes the protagonist appears to be winning, sometimes losing with the action increasing, then dropping off a little, only to become fiercer than ever. Throughout all of this the suspense increases about whether or not the protagonist will win or not.

The point at which the audience knows the central character will win or lose is called the play's climax.

The play's "story" actually may begin long before the play opens, but the playwright doesn't include all the events that are important to know. Instead, the writer presents these details, called the exposition, through dialog.

Exercises

1.   The antagonist does not always have to be another person. Sometimes it can be something inside the protagonist, such as too much pride. Sometimes it can be

a condition, such as living in a slum area, where there is a lot of pressure to take drugs or join a gang. In the scenes that follow, who is the protagonist and who or what are the antagonists? *(Exercises are continued on page 51.)*

1 # The Twelve-Pound Look
2 ## by James Barrie
3
4 *(This excerpt occurs a few minutes into the play. Harry*
5 *Sims, an Englishman, is to be knighted within a few*
6 *days. He has sent for a secretary to type letters answer-*
7 *ing people who sent notes and telegrams congratulat-*
8 *ing him on the knighthood. The action occurs in the*
9 *Sims' household. Mrs. Sims has just presented the*
10 *secretary to Harry. Notice that in this scene the stage*
11 *directions all indicate how Harry, the protagonist sees*
12 *things, and that they often mean just the opposite.)*
13
14 **SIR HARRY:** *(With concentrated scorn)* **You!**
15 **KATE:** *(As if agreeing with him)* **Yes, it's funny.**
16 **SIR HARRY:** **The shamelessness of your daring to**
17 **come here.**
18 **KATE:** **Believe me, it is not less a surprise to me**
19 **than it is to you. I was sent here in the ordinary**
20 **way of business. I was given only the number**
21 **of the house. I was not told the name.**
22 **SIR HARRY:** *(Withering her)* **The ordinary way of**
23 **business! This is what you have fallen to—a**
24 **typist!**
25 **KATE:** *(Unwithered)* **Think of it!**
26 **SIR HARRY:** **After going through worse straits, I'll**
27 **be bound.**
28 **KATE:** *(With some grim memories)* **Much worse**
29 **straits.**
30 **SIR HARRY:** *(Alas, laughing coarsely)* **My congratu-**

1   lations!

2   KATE: Thank you, Harry.

3   SIR HARRY: *(Who is annoyed, as any man would be,*

4   *not to find her abject)* **Eh? What is that you called**

5   **me, madam?**

6   KATE: Isn't it Harry? On my soul, I almost forgot.

7   SIR HARRY: It isn't Harry to you. My name is Sims,

8   if you please.

9   KATE: Yes, I had not forgotten that. It was my

10   name, too, you see.

11   SIR HARRY: *(In his best manner)* **It was your name**

12   **till you forfeited the right to bear it.**

13   KATE: Exactly.

14   SIR HARRY: *(Gloating)* **I was furious to find you**

15   **here, but on second thought it pleases me.** *(From*

16   *the depths of his moral nature)* **There is a grim**

17   **justice in this.**

18   KATE: *(Sympathetically)* **Tell me?**

19   SIR HARRY: Do you know what you were brought

20   here to do?

21   KATE: I have just been learning. You have been

22   made a knight, and I was summoned to answer

23   the messages of congratulation.

24   SIR HARRY: That's it, that's it. You come on this

25   day as my servant!

26   KATE: I, who might have been Lady Sims.

27   SIR HARRY: And you are her typist instead. And

28   she has four men-servants. Oh, I am so glad you

29   saw her in her presentation gown.

30   KATE: I wonder if she would let me do her washing,

31   Sir Harry? *(Her want of taste disgusts him.)*

32   SIR HARRY: *(With dignity)* **You can go. The mere**

33   **thought that only a few flights of stairs separates**

34   **such as you from my innocent children—** *(He will*

35   *never know why a new light has come into her face.)*

1   **KATE:** *(Slowly)* **You have children?**

2   **SIR HARRY:** *(Inflated)* **Two.** *(He wonders why she is*

3   *so long in answering.)*

4   **KATE:** *(Resorting to impertinence)* **Such a nice**

5   **number.**

6   **SIR HARRY:** *(With an extra turn of the screw)* **Both**

7   **boys.**

8   **KATE:** **Successful in everything. Are they like you,**

9   **Sir Harry?**

10   **SIR HARRY:** *(Expanding)* **They are very like me.**

11   **KATE:** **That's nice.** *(Even on such a subject as this she*

12   *can be ribald.)*

13   **SIR HARRY:** **Will you please to go?**

14   **KATE:** **Heighho. What shall I say to my employer?**

15   **SIR HARRY:** **That's no affair of mine.**

16   **KATE:** **What will you say to Lady Sims?**

17   **SIR HARRY:** **I flatter myself that whatever I say,**

18   **Lady Sims will accept without comment.** *(She*

19   *smiles, heaven knows why, unless her next remark*

20   *explains it.)*

21   **KATE:** **Still the same Harry.**

22   **SIR HARRY:** **What do you mean?**

23   **KATE:** **Only that you have the old confidence in**

24   **your profound knowledge of the sex.**

25   **SIR HARRY:** *(Beginning to think as little of her intellect*

26   *as of her morals)* **I suppose I know my wife.**

27   **KATE:** *(Hopelessly dense)* **I suppose so. I was only**

28   **remembering that you used to think you knew**

29   **her in the days when I was the lady.**

30

31

32   # The Closing of the Mine

33

34   *(In this scene Billy has just learned that Ruthie will*

35   *be moving. Both of the characters are age sixteen.)*

1   **SETTING:** The action takes place in Ruthie's living
2   room, which is filled with boxes of clothing, dishes
3   and books.
4
5   **BILLY:** *(Sitting on the sofa)* **Why didn't you tell me**
6   **you were moving?**
7   **RUTHIE:** *(Sitting beside BILLY)* **I just found out this**
8   **morning. At breakfast.** *(BILLY reaches for*
9   *RUTHIE's hand.)* **Oh, Billy, I don't want to move.**
10   **Not now. Not when I'm partway though my**
11   **junior year. I want to stay here and finish.** *(She*
12   *looks into his face.)* **There's a little grocery store**
13   **attached to the station. If people run out of**
14   **bread or milk, they can stop in.** *(Sighing)* **My**
15   **father's afraid. I can understand. There are still**
16   **three of us kids at home.**
17   **BILLY: But what about—**
18   **RUTHIE: I have to help finish packing. We're leav-**
19   **ing tomorrow afternoon.**
20   **BILLY: So soon?** *(Suddenly, he feels ashamed. He's*
21   *been thinking only of himself.)* **I'm going to miss**
22   **you. I'll miss you something terrible.**
23   **RUTHIE: It's not so far. Thirty or forty miles.**
24   **BILLY: I guess so. It just seems that everything's**
25   **falling apart.** *(He stands.)* **Will you write to me?**
26   **Let me know your address?**
27   **RUTHIE: Of course. I expect to hear from you too.**
28   **Do you understand?** *(She tries to laugh but can't.)*
29   **BILLY: What is it?**
30   **RUTHIE: We won't have to worry about which of**
31   **us goes to state band now, will we?** *(Suddenly,*
32   *she sobs, turns and runs up the stairs. BILLY stands*
33   *for a moment gazing up the flight of stairs, then turns*
34   *and exits Stage Left.)*
35

Script Writer

1
2
3 **SETTING:** The action takes place in the Hollywood
4   office of a big-time producer.
5 **CHARACTERS:** PRODUCER, fat, bald, always smok-
6   ing a cigar; MEL, just out of college, trying to be a
7   TV writer; SAMUEL, a body-builder type.
8
9 **MEL:** When will my script air?
10 **PRODUCER:** Well, now, I can't tell you that.
11 **MEL:** Hasn't it been scheduled?
12 **PRODUCER:** You don't understand.
13 **MEL:** I'm afraid I don't.
14 **PRODUCER:** *(Takes a few puffs of his cigar)* **What you**
15   **young fellows fail to realize is the impact of tele-**
16   **vision on the average person. It's the single**
17   **biggest influence of his life. In many cases it**
18   **becomes his life.**
19 **MEL:** What does that have to do with my script? I
20   thought you liked it. You said you were rushing
21   it into production.
22 **PRODUCER:** Don't rock the boat, kid.
23 **MEL:** I just want—
24 **PRODUCER:** *(Calling his male secretary)* **Samuel!**
25   *(SAMUEL enters.)* **Show Mr. Johns out. Im-**
26   **mediately.** *(SAMUEL grabs MEL's arm and forces*
27   *him out the door Stage Left.)*

(Exercises continued from page 47.)

2. You don't have to begin writing a play by building a
character. You can start with various other "bits and
pieces." For example:
    a. Think of a place you have seen recently for the first
       time. What kind of place is it? What sort of people
       do you think you would be likely to find there?
       Write a description of the scene and create at least

a couple of characters who logically could be there.

b. Think of an emotion such as disgust. Think of a reason for someone's being disgusted. Now create a character who is disgusted for this reason. What does the person say and do? To whom is he or she speaking? Where are they? Describe the environment and the circumstances. Now try the same thing with other emotions such as anger or jealousy.

c. Listen to a short conversation at school, at home or at a store. Now write down as much of it as you can remember. Then on paper extend the conversation another 60 seconds.

d. Develop a plot from a "saying" such as:
1. People who live in glass houses shouldn't throw stones.
2. A stitch in time saves nine.
3. A rolling stone gathers no moss.
4. Where there's a will there's a way.
5. Still water runs deep.

Think about what each of these sayings really means. Then from your idea develop characters, a setting and conflict. For example, a person wants very much to go to the school prom but has no money. He decides he will do whatever he can to be able to go. This, of course, is based on number four.

3. Now take one of the scenes you wrote as part of the exercises in this chapter and use it as part of something longer. Maybe the scene suggests further conflict or added characters. Write a new scene that either grows out of the scene you already wrote or else a scene that precedes it.

PART II
DIRECTING

CHAPTER FIVE
What Is a Director?

One of the most exciting jobs in theatre is that of director because this is the person who coordinates all the elements of a production. But before starting on a show, a director has a lot of preliminary work. First is analyzing the audience to try to figure out what sort of plays they would like. This is closely tied to the theatre's purpose, its reason for being in existence.

Audience Analysis

There are three basic reasons for theatre to exist, and the reasons match the three types of theatres: educational, community and professional. Educational theatre's purpose is to train people; community theatre's is to provide entertainment, and professional theatre's is to make money.

Educational Theatre

Although schools occasionally produce plays to raise money, usually the main purpose is to train students.

In many junior high and high schools the director is responsible for all aspects of a production from choosing the script to designing the scenery. In larger schools, the responsibilities are divided among several teachers.

Many colleges and universities, in addition to producing a season of four or more major productions, have experimental theatres where students can try their hands at whatever most interests them. Often they can choose or even write the plays. The major productions are planned by the entire theatre department, or, a committee made up of department members.

Some offer the opportunity for students to become apprentices with professional theatres.

Community Theatre

The purpose of most community theatres is to provide fun for both those working on a production and for the audience.

Although directors in a community theatre can offer suggestions for plays with which they would like to work, most community theatres have a play selection board or committee that chooses the season. They select what they think local audiences will like, most often recent Broadway hits or other popular plays.

Professional Theatre

There are many kinds of professional theatres, but for all of them the major purpose is to make money for the producers, people who raise the money to present a play.

Broadway producers are very careful about the plays they choose. Because it is very expensive to present a Broadway show, they can easily lose a lot of money. They try to choose plays that will continue to run for weeks, months or even years.

Off-Broadway is less expensive. According to Actors' Equity Association (the actors' union), an off-Broadway theatre cannot seat more than 299 spectators. If it were larger, it would have the potential to bring in more money. So the theatrical unions relax their rules on how much a person is to be paid.

Off-off-Broadway does much more experimenting with new ideas and new ways of presenting plays than does any other type of professional theatre. Productions, although often presented to make a profit, appeal to more limited audience members, with plays being presented in almost any sort of available space from lofts to churches.

There are many types of stock companies. Many use the same company throughout a season—usually summer—while others bring in recognized stars to play leading roles.

Professional theatre also includes dinner theatres, where a meal is served before the production, and touring productions of Broadway shows.

Choosing the Script

A lot of a theatre's success depends on the scripts they choose. This means the directors and producers have to give a lot of thought to what sort of people make up their potential audiences.

In San Diego, for instance, there is a professional group called Sledgehammer Theatre. There is another group called The San Diego Repertory Theatre. The Sledgehammer Theatre does plays that exist for reasons other than pure entertainment. The theatre's name was chosen to suggest "hitting people over the head" with theatre. The group has no permanent home, presenting their shows in a variety of locations. Although they are professional, they are not an Equity Theatre. That means they don't have to pay Equity wages, which generally are much higher. The group then can afford to do "heavy plays," such as the uncut version of *Hamlet*, which lasts much longer than most other full-length plays. They use highly imaginative designs, including bright lights shined into the audience's eyes, and costumes which are completely black with black makeup. They are appealing to a smaller audience rather than a large commercial theatre. Yet, in an area as large as San Diego, they do attract playgoers. They might not draw audiences in a rural area.

San Diego Repertory Theatre, on the other hand, has a permanent home in a city-owned theatre building in a large shopping center. They do some experimenting in their choice of plays, but have to be careful. They usually try to choose plays that they believe will draw large audiences. Many are strictly for entertainment, although they also do some that are more substantial in theme and content. A unique thing about the Repertory Theatre is that once a year they present a play in both Spanish and English. This works for them because they are close to Mexico and have a large Spanish-speaking population from which to draw.

Although drawing large audiences is not as big a concern for community and educational theatre as it is for professional theatre, the people who choose the scripts for production need to analyze potential audiences to see what will draw people to a performance.

Questions a producing organization needs to ask are:
1. What kind of audience do I want to reach?
2. Why do I want to reach this audience?
3. How do I go about reaching them?

The many financial failures on Broadway show that there is no sure-fire answer to these questions. Yet a director or a producer has a better success rate by keeping the audience in mind.

Directors need to figure out the age group they are appealing to. Is it a young high school or college audience, or a middle-aged audience, made up largely of business people, as is the usual case on Broadway? A director has a somewhat easier time in a large metropolitan area since there is a larger potential audience for every type of show than there would be in a rural area.

Exercises

1. Following are scenes from four plays. Read each of these scenes and decide the type of theatre in which you think

they would have the greatest chance of success. In which other types of theatres do you think they also could be presented? Discuss in class why you made the choices you did.

2. Take the same scenes and decide if there are any types of theatre in which these could not be presented. Again, discuss in class why you think as you do.

3. Take one of the scenes, choose a type of theatre in which you think it could succeed, and then figure out the potential audience. What age would they be? Why would they like the play? What would be their reasons for seeing it?

4. Choose which play you think your classmates would most enjoy. Make a list of reasons why you think so. Read the reasons to the class. See if they agree with the way you analyzed them.

An Enemy of the People
by Henrik Ibsen

1
2
3
4   *(The main character in the play is DR. STOCKMANN,*
5   *a scientist who has found that the water in the town*
6   *where he lives is being polluted by wastes from a*
7   *tannery owned by his father-in-law. At a public meet-*
8   *ing Stockmann tells what he has discovered, and the*
9   *townspeople turn against him since the public baths*
10 *provide a lot of income for the town. Despite this,*
11 *Stockmann still stands up for what he believes.*
12   *In this scene HOVSTAD and ASLAKSEN, a*
13 *newspaper editor and a printer, have heard that*
14 *Stockmann's father-in-law is buying up stock in the*
15 *baths, apparently hoping to make a profit. The two*
16 *men believe that once the father-in-law has all the*
17 *stock, Stockmann will declare the baths free of con-*
18 *tamination. They want a cut of any profits. Yet Stock-*
19 *mann is innocent of any scheming. This scene occurs*
20 *in Stockmann's house.)*
21 **DR. STOCKMANN: Well, what do you want with**

1   me? Be brief.
2   HOVSTAD: I can quite understand that you resent
3   our attitude at the meeting yesterday—
4   DR. STOCKMANN: Your attitude, you say. Yes, it
5   was a pretty attitude. I call it the attitude of
6   cowards—of old women— Shame on you!
7   HOVSTAD: Call it what you will, but we could not
8   act otherwise.
9   DR. STOCKMANN: You dared not, I suppose? Isn't
10   that so?
11   HOVSTAD: Yes, if you like to put it so.
12   ASLAKSEN: But why didn't you just say a word to
13   us beforehand? The merest hint to Mr. Hovstad
14   or to me?
15   DR. STOCKMANN: A hint? What about?
16   ASLAKSEN: About what was really behind it all.
17   DR. STOCKMANN: I don't in the least understand
18   you?
19   ASLAKSEN: *(Nods confidentially)* Oh, yes you do, Dr.
20   Stockmann.
21   HOVSTAD: It's no good making a mystery of it any
22   longer.
23   DR. STOCKMANN: *(Looking from one to the other)*
24   Why, what in the devil's name—?
25   ASLAKSEN: May I ask—isn't your father-in-law
26   going about the town buying up all the Bath
27   stock?
28   DR. STOCKMANN: Yes, he has been buying Bath
29   stock today but—
30   ASLAKSEN: It would have been more prudent to
31   let somebody else do that—someone not so
32   closely connected with you.
33   HOVSTAD: And then you ought not to have ap-
34   peared in the matter under your own name. No
35   one need have known that the attack on the

1   Baths came from you. You should have taken
2   me into your counsel, Dr. Stockmann.
3 DR. STOCKMANN: *(Stares straight in front of him; a*
4   *light seems to break in upon him, and he says as*
5   *though thunderstruck.)* **Is this possible? Can such**
6   things be?
7 ASLAKSEN: *(Smiling)* It's plain enough that they
8   can. But they ought to be managed delicately,
9   you understand.
10 HOVSTAD: And there ought to be more people in
11   it; for the responsibility always falls more lightly
12   when there are several to share it.
13 DR. STOCKMANN: *(Calmly)* In one word, gentle-
14   man—what is it you want?
15 ASLAKSEN: Mr. Hovstad can best—
16 HOVSTAD: No, you explain Aslaksen.
17 ASLAKSEN: Well, it's this: now that we know how
18   the matter really stands, we believe we can ven-
19   ture to place the *People's Messenger* at your
20   disposal.
21 DR. STOCKMANN: You can venture to now, eh?
22   But how about public opinion? Aren't you afraid
23   of bringing down a storm upon us?
24 HOVSTAD: We must manage to ride out the storm.
25 ASLAKSEN: And you must be ready to put about
26   quickly, Doctor. As soon as your attack has done
27   its work—
28 DR. STOCKMANN: As soon as my father-in-law
29   and I have bought up the shares at a discount,
30   you mean?
31 HOVSTAD: I presume it is mainly on scientific
32   grounds that you want to take the management
33   of the Baths into your own hands.
34 DR. STOCKMANN: Of course; it was on scientific
35   grounds that I got the old Badger to stand in

1   with me. And then we'll tinker up the water-
2   works a little, and potter about a bit down at
3   the beach, without its costing the town sixpence.
4   That ought to do the business. Eh?
5   HOVSTAD: I think so—if you have the *Messenger*
6   to back you.
7   ASLAKSEN: In free community the press is a
8   power, Doctor.
9   DR. STOCKMANN: Yes, indeed; and so is public
10   opinion. And you, Mr. Aslaksen—I suppose you
11   will answer for the House-owners' Association?
12   ASLAKSEN: Both for the House-owners' Associa-
13   tion and the Temperance Society. You may
14   make your mind easy.
15   DR. STOCKMANN: But gentlemen—really I'm
16   quite ashamed to mention such a thing—but—
17   what return—?
18   HOVSTAD: Of course, we should prefer to give you
19   our support for nothing. But the *Messenger* is
20   not very firmly established; it's not getting on
21   as it ought to, and I should be very sorry to have
22   to stop the paper just now, when there's so much
23   to be done in general politics.
24   DR. STOCKMANN: Naturally; that would be very
25   hard for a friend of the people like you. *(Flaring*
26   *up)* But I—I am an enemy of the people! *(Striding*
27   *about the room)* Where's my stick. Where the devil
28   is my stick?
29   HOVSTAD: What do you mean?
30   ASLAKSEN: Surely, you wouldn't—
31   DR. STOCKMANN: *(Standing still)* And suppose I
32   don't give you a single farthing out of all my
33   shares? You must remember we rich folks don't
34   like parting with our money.
35   HOVSTAD: And you must remember that this busi-

1   ness of the shares can be represented in two
2   ways.
3 DR. STOCKMANN: Yes, you are the man for that;
4   if I don't come to the rescue of the *Messenger,*
5   you'll manage to put a vile complexion on the
6   affair; you'll hunt me down, I suppose—bait
7   me—try to throttle me as a dog throttles a hare!
8 HOVSTAD: That's a law of nature—every animal
9   fights for its own subsistence.
10 ASLAKSEN: And must take its food where it can
11   find it, you know.
12 DR. STOCKMANN: Then see if you can't find some
13   out in the gutter; *(Striding about the room)* for
14   now, by heaven! we shall see which is the
15   strongest animal of us three. *(Finds his umbrella*
16   *and brandishes it.)* Now, look here—!
17 HOVSTAD: You surely don't mean to assault us!
18 ASLAKSEN: I say, be careful with that umbrella!
19 DR. STOCKMANN: Out at the window with you,
20   Mr. Hovstad!
21 HOVSTAD: *(By the hall door)* Are you utterly crazy?
22 DR. STOCKMANN: Out at the window, Mr. Aslak-
23   sen! Jump I tell you! Be quick about it!
24 ASLAKSEN: *(Running round the writing-table)* Mod-
25   eration, Doctor; I'm not at all strong; I can't
26   stand much— *(Screams)* Help! Help!
27
28
29   # Ties
30
31   *(This play is about two people who have been friends for*
32   *years. RANDY is staying for a few days taking care of*
33   *TOM who has just been released from the hospital where*
34   *he has been treated for a coronary.)*
35 **CHARACTERS:**   RANDY, 55; TOM, 70.

1   **SETTING:**   A tastefully decorated house in Del Mar,
2   California. The action takes place in the living room.
3   **AT RISE:**   TOM is seated in a chair near the fireplace.
4   Because he is still recovering from a serious coro-
5   nary, he wears felt slippers, silk pajamas and a velour
6   robe. He is reading the *L.A. Times.* RANDY enters
7   Upper Left and crosses to the sofa. He wears khaki
8   work pants, sneakers and a brown turtleneck.
9   **TOM:**   *(Shaking the paper to straighten the pages)* **Every**
10   **time I read the newspaper it scares me to death.**
11   **RANDY:**   **Then why don't you stop reading it?** *(He*
12   *flicks imaginary dust off the back of the sofa, circles*
13   *it and sits.)*
14   **TOM:**   *(Surprised)* **What?**
15   **RANDY:**   **You get yourself all worked up over noth-**
16   **ing. It's just plain stupid.**
17   **TOM:**   **For heaven's sake, Randy, don't you know**
18   **any day we could be blown up or get radiation**
19   **sickness from somebody messing up at some**
20   **stupid nuclear plant? It could happen. San**
21   **Onofre's not all that far away.** *(RANDY waves an*
22   *arm in an "aw, come on" gesture and leans back.)* **Or**
23   **air pollution. Sometimes you can look out the**
24   **window and see a filthy yellow mist hovering**
25   **over everything. Some morning we'll walk out-**
26   **side and not be able to breathe.**
27   **RANDY:**   **So what's different?**
28   **TOM:**   **I'm just reading the damned paper.**
29   **RANDY:**   **Fine then. Read your paper. Get yourself**
30   **all worked up.**
31   **TOM:**   **I am what I am, Randy, and I'll live with it.**
32   **Lord, man, I'm seventy years old. Why don't you**
33   **just face that?**
34   **RANDY:**   **No, you face it. You're the one's been sick.**
35   *(TOM carefully folds the newspaper and places it on*

1   *the nearest end table.)*
2   TOM: All right, what's this all about?
3   RANDY: What do you mean?
4   TOM: Oh, come on.
5   RANDY: *(Rises and crosses to the window.)* **I worry**
6   **about you, that's all. You don't take care of your-**
7   **self. You don't do what you're supposed to do.**
8   TOM: What do you want me to do? *(Rising and cross-*
9   *ing to the window)*
10   RANDY: You're my friend, Tom. I'm concerned
11   about you. *(The two men face each other, silhouetted*
12   *against the window.)*
13   TOM: I'm sorry, Randy. Whatever I've done, I'm
14   sorry.
15
16
17   # Carwash
18   ## by Louis Phillips
19
20   *CHARACTERS:*   KEN PFEIFFER, JOE WHISTLER,
21   DARLENE SILVERMAN.
22   *SETTING:*   In the dark we hear the sound of a carwash
23   at full throttle. The water hums a powerful spray,
24   the brushes create a concerto of scrub, the vacuum
25   cleaners vacuum, pulling dust and dirt out of some
26   kind of universe. The noise subsides. When the lights
27   come up on the Charm School Carwash, we see a few
28   buckets of soap, large sponges, two or three folding
29   chairs, dirty towels.
30   On-stage are two men. KEN PFEIFFER, who
31   is dressed in a dark suit and who is carrying a brief-
32   case, and JOE WHISTLER, a worker at the carwash.
33   JOE is in simple workpants, sneakers, and a white
34   shirt with the name: Charm School Carwash.
35   PFEIFFER: Get me the manager!

1   JOE: I am the manager.

2   PFEIFFER: No, you're not the manager. You're a
3   car thief.

4   JOE: Keep calm.

5   PFEIFFER: I am calm.

6   JOE: You're not calm.

7   PFEIFFER: You're not the manager.

8   JOE: I am one of the managers. Everyone on the
9   lot is a manager. It's part of a new psychological
10   theory of increasing profits. Make everybody
11   feel the way the owner feels. We learned it from
12   a book about the Japanese.

13   PFEIFFER: I don't want to hear about the
14   Japanese right now.

15   JOE: Why? Are they ruining your business too?

16   PFEIFFER: I don't have a business. And, at the
17   moment, I don't even have a car!

18   JOE: You have a car. You came in here with a car.
19   You will leave with one.

20   PFEIFFER: I want to leave with the one I came in
21   with.

22   JOE: You will.

23   PFEIFFER: Where is it?

24   JOE: It has to be in there somewhere.

25   PFEIFFER: It's not in there. I keep telling you. It's
26   not in there. Look! *(The owner of the carwash enters.*
27   *She is DARLENE SILVERMAN. In her midthirties,*
28   *she is short, with frizzled hair. She wears a blue*
29   *jumpsuit.)*

30   DARLENE: What seems to be the trouble here?

31   PFEIFFER: I want the manager.

32   DARLENE: I am the manager.

33   PFEIFFER: Of course. Everbody's a manager in
34   this business. It's something you learned from
35   the Japanese. . . .

1   DARLENE: What's that supposed to mean?

2   JOE: He's upset because he lost his car.

3   DARLENE: He lost his car?

4   JOE: He lost his car.

5   PFEIFFER: I lost my car.

6   DARLENE: You lost your car?

7   PFEIFFER: What are we talking about here?

8   JOE: I thought we were talking about losing your
9   car.

10   PFEIFFER: That's right. That's exactly what I'm
11   talking about. Losing my car.

12   DARLENE: If you lost your car, what are you doing
13   at a carwash? It doesn't make any sense to come
14   to a carwash without a car.

15   PFEIFFER: Are you crazy? What are you talking
16   about? I came here with my car. And now I don't
17   have a car. I put it in there. *(Points to the carwash*
18   *tunnel.)*

19   DARLENE: *(To JOE)* What's he talking about?

20   JOE: He lost his car.

21   DARLENE: He lost his car?

22   PFEIFFER: I lost my car . . . in there.

23   DARLENE: Is this some kind of a joke? You lost
24   your car in there?

25   PFEIFFER: I didn't lose the car. You lost the car.

26   DARLENE: *(To JOE)* What's he talking about? It's
27   impossible to lose a car in there.

28   PFEIFFER: You did something to it.

29   JOE: I didn't touch the car.

30   PFEIFFER: Somebody touched the car!

31   JOE: I don't touch the cars until they come out of
32   the tunnel. Your car didn't come out of the tun-
33   nel. Therefore, I didn't touch it.

34   DARLENE: *(To PFEIFFER)* See?

35   PFEIFFER: See what?

1 DARLENE: He didn't touch your car. So what are
2   you complaining about?
3 PFEIFFER: What am I complaining about?
4 JOE: What's he complaining about?
5 PFEIFFER: Stop it! I didn't want you trying any of
6   your charm school stuff on me.
7 JOE: What charm school stuff?
8 PFEIFFER: I didn't find any of it charming.
9 DARLENE: I still don't understand what you're
10   complaining about.
11 PFEIFFER: I told you.
12 DARLENE: You didn't tell me.
13 PFEIFFER: I drove my car into this Charm School
14   and Carwash . . .
15 DARLENE: It's not charm school and carwash. It's
16   Charm School Carwash. It's owned by a woman
17   named Charm School.
18 PFEIFFER: There's actually a woman named
19   Charm School?
20 DARLENE: Of course there is. You don't think that
21   we would actually name a carwash Charm
22   School unless the owner wanted her name upon
23   it. But maybe you think it's funny to make fun
24   of a person's name.
25 PFEIFFER: Are you the owner?
26 DARLENE: No, I'm the manager.
27 JOE: One of the managers.
28
29
30 # Christopher Puppy
31
32 *CHARACTERS:* CHRISTOPHER, 4, played by an
33   adult who pretends. MOTHER, an adult who doesn't
34   pretend.
35 *SETTING:* The action occurs in CHRISTOPHER's

```
 1      house early on a spring morning.
 2      (CHRISTOPHER comes into the kitchen rubbing
 3      sleep from his eyes.)
 4
 5   MOTHER:   Good morning, Christopher.
 6   CHRISTOPHER:   Bow wow. I'm a puppy. (MOTHER
 7      sets a bowl on the table.) Puppies have more fun
 8      than little boys.
 9   MOTHER:   (Laughing) All right. Now sit down at the
10      table. Breakfast will be ready soon.
11   CHRISTOPHER:   (Dropping to his hands and knees)
12      Bow wow.
13   MOTHER:   Oh, I see. (She goes to the cupboard and
14      brings back a big dog biscuit.)
15   CHRISTOPHER:   Grrr. Grrr.
16   MOTHER:   What's the matter? Don't you like your
17      breakfast?
18   CHRISTOPHER:   Grrr.
```

Working with the Other Artists

The only theatre artist who sometimes does not collaborate directly with the other artists is the playwright. But this is true only if the play already has been published.

In premiere productions of a play, the writer often attends rehearsals and rewrites scenes and dialog on the basis of whether it seems to be working well or not. The director and the designers may even suggest changes in the script to make the production more effective.

In most theatres the director is the one who has the final say in all aspects of production. The producer may also make suggestions, but it is the director who has the final responsibility for how the production comes across.

Of course, all directors work differently because they have different personalities and so don't all approach their jobs in the same way. Some directors like to develop an overall concept before they even meet with the designers. Others allow the costumers and the set and lighting designers to come up with suggestions before revealing thoughts they have about a show.

It is logical that the director or at least someone have the final word so that all the areas of design are coordinated.

A professional costume designer, Patricia Zipprodt, has explained this by saying that she feels the designers are "creative extensions" of the director. She says that designers are the people who make the world in which the characters "live."

As she says, designers visually "supplement" the director's concept. All the work has to mesh, so that, for instance, blue light would not be used, except for a special effect, on red costuming, or the costuming would appear black to the audience.

Directors thus wear many hats: They are artists, teachers, organizers and technicians. They have to be able to work well with other people and communicate their ideas.

Most often to be able to do these things directors have a lot of experience and training in theatre. Just as playwrights must understand the workings of theatre to write a workable play, directors have to be well-acquainted with all areas so they can understand what will work and what will not. They have to understand the problems of design, as well as understanding human nature. They have to know the art of acting in order to guide the performers.

Besides all that, they have to learn how to manage the finances of a production and stay within an allotted budget.

Directing is a big job, involving a tremendous amount of work and dedication. But it also is a rewarding job, particularly when everything meshes.

Exercises

1. Work together in groups of three. One person plays the role of director, one the role of costume and make-up designer, the other the role of set and lighting designer. Now choose one of the scenes in this chapter and together decide on how you would design the play, coordinating all the areas. Report to the rest of the class on what you decided.

2. If you were the director of one of the scenes in this chapter, what would you change about the script—to make it more interesting, funnier, clearer or just better. Not changing anything is okay too. But be able to say why you think the script works well as it is.

CHAPTER SIX
Interpreting a Script

Interpreting the Play

Long before casting the show or meeting with the other theatre artists, the director begins working. This preliminary work involves analyzing the script and interpreting the play.

The Central Idea

One of the first steps is to figure out the theme or central idea, the playwright's purpose in writing the play. The reason is to be certain that the production emphasizes what the playwright intended. Some central ideas are easy to figure out. For instance, in *The Closing of the Mine*, the central idea could be: All of us experience painful changes in our lives.

One director, however, may come up with a different central idea, a different message he or she believes the playwright is communicating. This is all right if the director can "prove" the idea through pointing to things in the play that support what he or she believes. For instance, a different central idea for *The Closing of the Mine* could be: Growing to maturity is a painful process.

Either of the two interpretations could be justified since the play deals with a young man going through change, which is a painful thing. But one director may see it simply as the pain of adolescence, while another sees it as the pain we suffer throughout our lives.

Keep in mind that not all central ideas are as easy to figure out. In many cases the playwright is speaking metaphorically, that is, he or she is using symbolism or comparisons to communicate the theme. In *Waiting for Godot* the characters are gathered waiting for someone to appear. Whoever it is never comes. Most people think this is symbolic, that is, it stands for another thing. Some say it symbolizes waiting for the second coming of Jesus Christ. Others say the playwright meant to show only that much of our lives are spent in waiting for things that never happen.

Exercises

1. What do you think is the central idea of the following short play? Be able to tell the rest of the class why you think so.
2. Did anyone else come up with a different interpretation? If so, do you agree or disagree with what the other person said? Be prepared to tell the class why you feel as you do.

1	**Anniversary**
2	**by Conrad Bishop and Elizabeth Fuller**
3	**First produced by The Independent Eye**
4	
5	*CHARACTERS:* The MAN—Chris; the WOMAN—
6	Chris's wife.
7	*SETTING:* The action takes place in the present in the
8	home of a sophisticated young couple celebrating
9	their first anniversary. The room has an intimate
10	dining table and two chairs. A telephone sits on a
11	nearby end table.
12	
13	MAN: Terrific meal.
14	WOMAN: For a terrific couple.
15	MAN: Happy anniversary, honey.
16	WOMAN: The first of many.
17	MAN: Many happy returns.
18	WOMAN: Speaking of returns, do you want to look
19	at the bills?
20	MAN: This is our anniversary, honey.
21	WOMAN: There's a final notice.
22	MAN: Yeh, but . . .
23	WOMAN: I'll put them on the desk.
24	MAN: So many things have happened in one year.

1   So many adjustments.

2   WOMAN: Adjusting, learning to give and take . . .

3   MAN: Take charge of our lives, face up to our prob-

4   lems and solve them.

5   WOMAN: And now that we've solved them, it

6   should really be nice.

7   MAN: Because it has been kind of rough, you

8   know . . .

9   WOMAN: Well sure, it's hard to grow. We've grown

10   personally.

11   MAN: We have. Like our quarrels have grown . . . I

12   mean they've matured.

13   WOMAN: Our anger, we've learned how to deal

14   with it. That magazine article . . .

15   MAN: "Have Fun with Your Anger."

16   WOMAN: And you know, when we have kids, I am

17   never going to be angry with them. It's just not

18   necessary. If you love them and raise them the

19   right way, they'll never cause you problems.

20   MAN: Not many couples could say on their first an-

21   niversary that they have solved all their signifi-

22   cant problems.

23   WOMAN: But it's true.

24   MAN: I think we're way ahead of most couples.

25   Maybe five years ahead of most.

26   WOMAN: Happy anniversary, honey. *(They kiss and*

27   *turn front.)* Our marriage, well it's hard to talk

28   about because it really has been this incredible

29   experience . . .

30   MAN: Incredible but believable. We're more than

31   just married. We're good friends.

32   WOMAN: Friends, of course we're more than just

33   friends. It's so stimulating, so liberating . . . I've

34   been liberated to do so much. New furniture,

35   new colors, new recipes . . .

1   MAN: Zulu cookery. We have so many tastes in com-
2   mon. Even colors. Now the brighter end of the
3   chartreuse scale is not often . . .
4   WOMAN: It's not often found so early in a marriage.
5   MAN: Really incredible. *(They turn to one another.)*
6   WOMAN: Honey, before it gets too late and we get
7   involved in something else, could you take out
8   the garbage?
9   MAN: Huh?
10   WOMAN: Would you take out the garbage? It's kind
11   of piled up.
12   MAN: Honey . . . you're gonna laugh.
13   WOMAN: What?
14   MAN: The garbage. I just can't cope with the gar-
15   bage.
16   WOMAN: Oh. Well, as long as it's out before break-
17   fast.
18   MAN: No. I don't mean garbage now. I mean gar-
19   bage always. Garbage forever.
20   WOMAN: But we agreed: garbage is your province.
21   Do you think we're making too much garbage,
22   is that it?
23   MAN: It's not a recycling question, or a question of
24   less garbage or better garbage. It's the fact of
25   garbage.
26   WOMAN: Well, it's a human fact. We all generate
27   refuse. If you put two people together . . .
28   MAN: That's it. That's it. This is our product. Our
29   love, our sensitivity, our relationship results in
30   this . . . horrible accumulation. Oh, I know it's a
31   petty little thing, but . . .
32   WOMAN: It's not petty. There *are* three sacks of it.
33   Honey, this is our anniversary. I would like it
34   to be a garbage-free anniversary.
35   MAN: And how can we really, truly say Happy

1   Anniversary when there is this external man-
2   ifestation of our relationship bulging across the
3   kitchen at us? The Johnsons? Two doors down?
4   He goes out once a week with a little plastic
5   thing. It doesn't look like garbage, it doesn't
6   smell like garbage. It's an intense but com-
7   prehensible concentration of semi-organic sub-
8   stance, like the Johnsons. But ours . . .
9 WOMAN: I don't understand.
10 MAN: Take out the garbage. Please. *You* take out
11   the garbage.
12 WOMAN: I could take out the garbage.
13 MAN: Yes.
14 WOMAN: But I think there's something more basic
15   here.
16 MAN: Honey . . .
17 WOMAN: Why do you want to give *me* the garbage
18   when you hate it so much?
19 MAN: I'm not giving it to you.
20 WOMAN: I just don't like the idea of having it thrust
21   into my hands.
22 MAN: I'm not thrusting.
23 WOMAN: You are thrusting.
24 MAN: Why do you use these masculine images? I'm
25   not trying to thrust it, I'm trying to . . . *share*
26   it! . . . You've never had the freedom to take out
27   the garbage, and I want that experience *for you.*
28 WOMAN: Well . . . thank . . . you . . . *(They turn front.)*
29   It is a dilemma, of course, not that it can't be
30   worked out. I have a great concern for the gar-
31   bage, just as much as Chris does, because it
32   seems to have this place of importance in our
33   lives . . .
34 MAN: It's a kind of focal point for a lot of things,
35   and maybe if we can just focus on the focal point,

1   things will come more into focus.
2 WOMAN: Because very often, in terms of taking re-
3   sponsibility, Chris has a tendency to . . . give it
4   to me. And we thought perhaps we should work
5   this out the way we work things out. He would
6   state what he feels and I would state what I feel.
7   Which we did. I stated that the garbage needs
8   taking out.
9 MAN: And I agreed. But I stated that I had a very
10   negative reaction to her tone of voice in stating
11   her statement.
12 WOMAN: So I tried to find a better tone of voice in
13   which to state the needs of the garbage, in order
14   to strike a better balance between Chris's needs
15   and those of the garbage. I tried a plain old
16   "Take out the garbage."
17 MAN: That's very blunt.
18 WOMAN: OK. "Honey, I wonder if I might ask you
19   to expel the garbage?"
20 MAN: It rings false.
21 WOMAN: OK. "Sweetheart. Dearest. I know you
22   don't like to, because there's a lot on your mind
23   such as solving the nation's balance of payments
24   and also paying our bills, but I really don't know
25   where to put any more garbage. Should I pile it
26   in the bathroom or the closets, or put it in the
27   bed as a helpful hint, or serve it again for dinner?
28   Or maybe we could sleep in the garage and use
29   the house for the garbage, but could you *please*
30   *take it out?* "
31 MAN: I hate attempts at humor.
32 WOMAN: "Oh, look at *this!* It's the *garbage!* It would
33   be so much fun to do something with this! But
34   I need a big, strong man to do it! And everyone
35   will look out their window and say, 'What a big,

1   **strong man going down those stairs! Doesn't he**
2   **take good care of her garbage!' "**
3   MAN: She really misses the whole point.
4   WOMAN: "Hey baby, haul my garbage!" . . . Not to
5   take away from our anniversary . . .
6   MAN: Because it really is a very happy anniversary,
7   really . . .
8   WOMAN: Really, really, really incredible. *(They turn*
9   *to one another and start to laugh.)*
10   MAN: I don't know how we got into this.
11   WOMAN: Neither do I.
12   MAN: I mean I don't think it's really a problem. It's
13   just a new aspect of our relationship.
14   WOMAN: Though it is an aspect that's beginning to
15   pile up.
16   MAN: Look. I'm not trying to shove it under the rug.
17   WOMAN: No way, no way. Let's put it out in the
18   *middle* of the rug. Some people have potted
19   plants, we'll have canned fungus. The mold will
20   just match the color scheme . . . Go on. Say some-
21   thing.
22   MAN: No.
23   WOMAN: Don't repress it.
24   MAN: I have to repress it.
25   WOMAN: You don't have to repress it.
26   MAN: You make me repress it.
27   WOMAN: I just said it: Don't repress it. Don't re-
28   press it.
29   MAN: But your attitude is repress it, repress it.
30   WOMAN: OK then, repress it! Only repress it better!
31   MAN: Look, we both know that in order to be re-
32   solved this has to come out some way, and not
33   destructively, of course, but in a constructive
34   way that will bring us closer together . . .
35   WOMAN: OK then *do it! Do it! Do it!*

1 MAN: OK. OK. OK. I'm sick of it all, and it has noth-
2 ing to do with the garbage. It's you and the job
3 and the marriage. I want to throw up. I want to
4 break every window in this mousetrap house. I
5 want to get in the car and take off ninety miles
6 an hour to California and forget I ever got in
7 this because I can't stand the thought of fifty
8 more years of the same damn thing. I want to
9 give all the wedding presents to Goodwill, and
10 you come at me with this earnest little mousy
11 sarcastic whine and patch it up with one sincere
12 conversation a week, and we make a list that
13 we lose under all the garbage we spew out day
14 and night and I'm sick of it all! . . . Wow. I feel
15 better.
16 WOMAN: You do?
17 MAN: Yes. I feel good. Do you feel good?
18 WOMAN: No.
19 MAN: We have a better understanding.
20 WOMAN: Can I react to that?
21 MAN: I don't need a reaction.
22 WOMAN: You . . . *insensitive . . . insincere . . . in-*
23 *secure . . . immature . . .* *(Phone rings.)*
24 MAN: Telephone.
25 WOMAN: *(She answers it. Total change of tone)*
26 Hello? . . . Linda, hi! Oh nothing, just celebrating
27 our anniversary. Talking things over, making
28 plans.
29 MAN: Tell her about the house.
30 WOMAN: We looked at a new house. It's incredible!
31 Big lawn, carpets, all electric . . . George wants
32 to say Happy Anniversary.
33 MAN: . . . Yeah, made it through the first. Fifty more
34 to go. Yeah, incredible. Everything is incredible.
35 Appreciate it. Yeah. Bye. *(Hangs up. Silence)*

1   WOMAN: Nice of them to call.

2   MAN: We called them on theirs. *(Long silence)* **When**

3   **do you want to see the lawyer?**

4   WOMAN: I'll call Monday.

5   MAN: You use ours. I'll find a new one.

6   WOMAN: Everything should be fifty-fifty.

7   MAN: Even the garbage.

8   WOMAN: It's good we can be mature about things.

9   MAN: Make a rational judgment before we

10   get . . . too involved.

11   WOMAN: You want me to pack you something?

12   MAN: No, I'll stop by tomorrow.

13   WOMAN: You know, I think we still are way, way

14   ahead. A lot of couples, it takes, oh, six or seven

15   years before they split. We've saved all those

16   years.

17   MAN: I wonder what would happen . . . if one of

18   us . . . sort of . . .

19   WOMAN: Gave in? Compromised?

20   MAN: Probably . . . set a bad precedent. . . . Well,

21   happy . . .

22   WOMAN: Yes . . . happy . . . *(They shake hands. Si-*

23   *lence)* **Incredible.**

Some directors work out their interpretations of the play in detail before meeting with the designers and actors. Others work more closely with their colleagues in planning the production. Yet each production of a play is different from any other because the directors are different and so are their interpretations of the script.

Figuring Out the Climax

After determining the central idea, the next step is to figure out where the major and minor climaxes occur and how they can be emphasized.

In the following scene, although the action is silly, you can see where the highpoints occur.

1   *from* **We Are, You Are, They Are**
2
3   *CHARACTERS:* PROFESSOR, JUNE, DOTTY, JIM,
4   SALLY, BILL.
5   *SETTING:* A university classroom with a desk for the profes-
6   sor and desks for the students. The time is the present.
7   *(JUNE enters. She is a typical coed. She glances shyly*
8   *around the room and beckons for silence.)*
9
10   **JUNE:** *(Apologetically)* **I came as quickly as I could. How-**
11   **ever, the tidings I bring are not at all happy ones.**
12   **PROFESSOR:** *(Concerned)* **What is it, my child?**
13   **JUNE: War has been declared.**
14   **DOTTY, JIM, SALLY, BILL, PROFESSOR:** *(Simultane-*
15   *ously)* **War?**
16   **JUNE: I told you it wasn't pretty. Yes, war. Civil war.**
17   **War between the North and the South.**
18   **PROFESSOR: When?**
19   **BILL: How?**
20   **JUNE: As to how, I don't know. As to when, it was exactly**
21   *(Pause)* **some period or other during the eighteen hun-**
22   **dreds.**
23   **JIM:** *(Bravely)* **Damn the torpedoes! I've just begun to**
24   **fight.**
25   **SALLY: Will you go, Jim?**
26   **DOTTY: Will you go, Bill?**
27   **JIM: When duty calls, we just go.**
28   **BILL: We must go.**
29   **JUNE: There's no need for that.**
30   **PROFESSOR:** *(The inspired patriot)* **No need. Why, girl,**
31   **I've been thinking of joining up myself.**
32   **JIM: The war is over; the battle's won. Appomattox**
33   **and all that. General Grant is victorious.**
34   **BILL: Hallelujah!**
35   **PROFESSOR: Praises be! I didn't really fancy myself**
36   **fighting on some distant battleground, and for what?**

1   JIM: For what?

2   DOTTY: For what?

3   SALLY: We don't want to be embroiled in some petty

4   war. Peace, peace at any cost.

5   PROFESSOR: It's a hard decision to make, and why?

6   JIM: Yes, why—to protect the world from the spread

7   of . . . a vile, devouring monster. We shall not go.

8   JUNE: But the war is over now. Brother against brother.

9   Man against man.

10   PROFESSOR: And now the end has come. *(In near panic)*

11   Why wasn't I informed? Why wasn't I informed?

12   JUNE: I did my best.

13   PROFESSOR: You're not to be blamed. To err is human,

14   to forgive is to forget.

15   SALLY: *(A sincere compliment)* Nobly said. Nobly said.

16   JUNE: And now if you don't mind, professor, I must

17   spread my tidings elsewhere.

18   PROFESSOR: I understand. *(The frustrated actor)* Let not

19   the light burn out. Through sleet and hail and storm

20   of night, remember always keep it bright.

21   JUNE: *(Melodramatic)* You bring a sob to my throat, a

22   tear to my eye.

23   DOTTY: Such sentimental garbage.

24   JUNE: For you, maybe. But not for me. Because I always

25   keep this thought before me. *(She sweeps to the door.)*

26   Henry Ford mass-produced cars. *(She exits.)*

Overall, the play pokes fun at education—both at the faculty and the students. Then in individual scenes it deals with other themes as well. Here the scene is about the supposedly civilized person's view of war, sentimental patriotism on one hand and pacifism on the other. Yet everyone except June is totally misinformed. This is pointed up by the silliness of both the professor and the students not knowing the Civil War was fought many years ago. And even June who knows it was fought in the 1800s apparently does not realize that she therefore does not need to provide "war bulletins."

The scene begins with an inciting incident, where June

comes to tell the others about the war. Everyone becomes excited, which makes the action build with the men all wanting to "join up." A minor climax is reached when June says: "The war is over." Everyone's actions and lines seem to indicate that they have accepted what she says. Then, however, a few lines later they seem to have forgotten this and their attitudes switch from wanting to join to deciding not to become involved, no matter what.

Another minor climax is reached when the professor again seems to accept what June has said: "You're not to be blamed. To err is human, to forgive is to forget" (of course, mixing up two common sayings).

The scene ends nonsensically, going back to the play's major theme which is that much of formal education is silly and pretentious.

The Prevailing Mood

Plays should have an overall mood. Even though the mood may change somewhat from scene to scene, at the end of the play an audience should not be confused about what they are expected to feel. Shakespeare used "comic relief," brief scenes of comedy, in his tragedies although everyone knows without any doubt that *Hamlet* is a tragedy. The idea is that it is hard to sustain a tragic mood throughout an entire play. And besides if the mood is broken, the audience, as a result of the contrast, will feel an even greater sense of the tragic.

As you learned, there are some plays, tragicomedies, where the playwright wants the audience to be confused. Then it becomes even more shocking to learn that something that came across as funny really was not funny at all. The point of this sort of writing is that life itself is a mixture of the funny and the serious and a play should reflect life.

But even when working with a tragicomedy, the director has to know which mood to emphasize and what mood the audience should be left with.

In the following, what is the overall or prevailing mood? What makes you think so?

1   *from* **Two Gentlemen of Verona**
2   **by William Shakespeare**
3
4   *(Enter JULIA and LUCETTA.)*
5   **JULIA: But say, Lucetta, now we are alone,**
6   **Wouldst thou, then, counsel me to fall in love?**

1   LUCETTA: Aye, Madam, so you stumble not unheedfully.
2   JULIA: Of all the fair resort[1] of gentlemen
3   That every day with parle[2] encounter me,
4   In thy opinion which is worthiest love?
5   LUCETTA: Please you repeat their names, I'll show my
6   mind
7   According to my shallow simple skill.
8   JULIA: What think'st thou of the fair Sir Eglamour?
9   LUCETTA: As of a knight well-spoken, neat and fine;
10   But were I you, he never should be mine.
11 JULIA: What think'st thou of the rich Mercatio?
12 LUCETTA: Well of his wealth, but of himself, so so.
13 JULIA: What think'st though of the gentle Proteus?
14 LUCETTA: Lord, Lord! To see what folly reigns in us!
15 JULIA: How now! What means this passion[3] at his name?
16 LUCETTA: Pardon, dear madam. 'Tis a passing shame
17   That I, unworthy body as I am,
18   Should censure[4] thus on lovely gentlemen.
19 JULIA: Why not on Proteus, as of all the rest?
20 LUCETTA: Then thus—of many good I think him best.
21 JULIA: Your reason?
22 LUCETTA: I have no other but a woman's reason.
23   I think him so, because I think him so.
24 JULIA: And wouldst thou have me cast my love on him?
25 LUCETTA: Aye, if you thought your love not cast away.
26 JULIA: Why, he, of all the rest, hath never moved[5] me.
27 LUCETTA: Yet he, of all the rest, I think, best loves ye.
28 JULIA: His little speaking shows his love but small.
29 LUCETTA: Oh, they love least that let men know their
30   love.
31 JULIA: I would I knew his mind.
32 LUCETTA: Peruse this paper, madam.

[1]party of visitors
[2]talk
[3]emotion
[4]criticize
[5]conversed with

1 JULIA: "To Julia."— Say, from whom?
2 LUCETTA: That the contents will show.
3 JULIA: Say, say, who gave it thee?
4 LUCETTA: Sir Valentine's page, and sent, I think, from
5   Proteus.
6   He would have given it you, but I, being in the way,[6]
7   Did in your name receive it. Pardon the fault, pray.
8 JULIA: Now, by my modesty, a goodly broker![7]
9   Dare you presume to harbor wanton lines?
10   To whisper and conspire against my youth?
11   Now, trust me, 'tis an office of great worth.
12   And you take an officer fit for the place.
13   There, take the paper. See it be returned,
14   Or else return no more into my sight.
15 LUCETTA: To plead for love deserves more fee than
16   hate.
17 JULIA: Will you be gone?
18 LUCETTA: That you may ruminate. *(Exit)*

This play is the story of how a faithless man makes love to the fiancée of his best friend. There is disagreement over whether or not Shakespeare meant anyone to take the events of the play seriously. If you interpret the scene as a gentle mockery of the idea of romantic love, the play is humorous. If not, the play has a more serious tone.

Analyzing the Characters

The next step is to try to understand the characters, their relationships, and how they feel about each other. For instance, one character may dominate another. The domination defines the relationship. In addition, the one being dominated may like being protected or, on the other hand, may be resentful about it. This is the feeling.

As a director you also need to figure out the most important traits of the major characters in order for them to come across clearly to an audience. Next you should determine how the charac-

[6]meeting him
[7]go-between

ters fit into the play as a whole. What is their purpose, and how do they help advance the plot?

Every character should be included for a reason. You can think of this in terms of needs or goals. What is the character trying to get? What does he or she need in each scene? In the scene in chapter five from *An Enemy of the People*, for instance, Aslaksen wants to make money from the closing and reopening of the baths. This tells us something about his character, that he is dishonest, since he believes Stockmann is simply using a "scam" to make money for his father-in-law and himself. In the same scene, Stockmann seems to be playing along with Aslaksen and Hovstad but is simply trying to find out what they really want. So his goal is the same as throughout the rest of the play—to protect an unsuspecting public from illness because of the contaminated baths.

You need to know what it is about each character that brings him or her into conflict with other characters. Why do the protagonist and the antagonist oppose each other?

How is each character unique? How does each possess universal qualities and what are these qualities?

You have to decide which character or characters are most important in each scene and how this can be pointed up for the audience. You also decide which lines are most important in each scene and how these lines advance the plot. This is so that during the blocking you can figure out how to place the actors and how to have them move to best emphasize the important lines.

Another consideration is the subject matter of the play and why it would be important to an audience. For instance, in *We Are, You Are, They Are*, the subject matter is education and student-teacher relationships. The silly lines point this up, but the director has to figure out how these lines can be effectively presented to an audience so the idea comes across. Even though the play is funny, it has a serious purpose in saying that education is not always what it should be and so needs to be changed. How can a director make certain that this is communicated to an audience? The answer is by making sure the audience does not miss the most important lines. This is done partly by placement of the actors, much the way soloists in a concert band sometimes stand to have the attention directed toward them.

Determining the Setting and Atmosphere

At this point, some directors may want to meet with the designers to begin planning the setting. Others will first want to think about the setting themselves.

Sometimes the director's interpretation greatly influences the designers' ideas. This is especially true when the director figures out a strong metaphor for the play. A metaphor is a comparison that fits the production overall. For instance, in *We Are, You Are, They Are*, the director may decide to bring out the idea that a classroom is like a zoo. In that case, he or she might want the designers to make the setting suggest a cage, and maybe even have the characters wear make-up and costumes that hint at the idea that each student is to represent a different animal.

Or going along with the silliness of the play, the director may decide that this classroom is like a circus with each character a sort of clown. Choosing a metaphor for a play is taking something suggested in the script and enlarging on it.

Directors use a *prompt book* in which they include their plans for the production. The prompt book has the script in the middle of large pages, usually typing paper size, to allow margins for notes. One of the first things they may include is an analysis sheet like this:

Director's Analysis Sheet

Play _____

Playwright _____

Theme or Central Idea:

Metaphor:

Character Descriptions:

    Character 1

    Character 2

Character 3

Character 4

Character 5

The Goals of Each Character:

The Importance of Each Character:

The Basic Struggle or Conflict:

The Needs of Each Character:

Diagram of the set, showing placement of furniture and other set pieces:

Exercises

1. What kind of setting would you like to use for the following scene? What kind of lighting? Make-up? Costuming? The play is a portrait of the common people of Ireland. It uses poetic dialog in showing a mother's grief over the loss of her husband and sons. The playwright deals strongly with the idea of grief.
2. Figure out the most important traits of the characters and how they feel about each other. Also figure out their goals, what each is working toward or wants in the scene.
3. Which are the most important lines? Why? Discuss all these things with the rest of the class.

1 # Riders to the Sea
2 ### by John Millington Synge
3
4 *CHARACTERS:* MAURYA, the mother; CATHLEEN,
5 a daughter; NORA, a daughter.
6 *(At the beginning of the scene MAURYA is keening,*
7 *that is crying rhythmically. CATHLEEN is using a*
8 *spinning wheel.)*
9
10 **CATHLEEN:** Did you see him riding down?
11 *(MAURYA goes on keening. CATHLEEN—A little*
12 *impatiently)* **God forgive you; isn't it a better**
13 **thing to raise your voice and tell what you seen,**
14 **than to be making lamentation for a thing that's**
15 **done? Did you see Bartley, I'm saying to you.**
16 **MAURYA:** *(With a weak voice)* **My heart's broken**
17 **from this day.**
18 **CATHLEEN:** *(As before)* **Did you see Bartley?**
19 **MAURYA:** **I seen the fearfulest thing.**
20 **CATHLEEN:** *(Leaves her wheel and looks out.)* **God for-**
21 **give you; he's riding the mare now over the**
22 **green head, and the gray pony behind him.**
23 **MAURYA:** *(Starts, so that her shawl falls back from her*

1   *head and shows her white tossed hair. With a*

2   *frightened voice)* **The gray pony behind him.**

3   **CATHLEEN:** *(Coming to the fire)* **What is it ails you,**

4   **at all?**

5   **MAURYA:** *(Speaking very slowly)* **I've seen the fear-**

6   **fulest thing any person has seen, since the day**

7   **Bride Dara seen the dead man with a child in**

8   **his arms.**

9   **CATHLEEN and NORA:** **Uah.** *(They crouch down in*

10   *front of the old woman at the fire.)*

11   **NORA:** **Tell us what it is you seen.**

12   **MAURYA:** **I went down to the spring well, and I**

13   **stood there saying a prayer to myself. Then**

14   **Bartley came along, and he riding on the red**

15   **mare with the gray pony behind him.** *(She puts*

16   *her hands, as if to hide something from her eyes.)*

17   **The Son of God spare us, Nora!**

18   **CATHLEEN:** **What is it you seen?**

19   **MAURYA:** **I seen Michael himself.**

20   **CATHLEEN:** *(Speaking softly)* **You did not, Mother;**

21   **it wasn't Michael you seen, for his body is after**

22   **being found in the Far North, and he's got a**

23   **clean burial by the grace of God.**

24   **MAURYA:** *(A little defiantly)* **I'm after seeing him this**

25   **day, and he riding and galloping. Bartley came**

26   **first on the red mare; and I tried to say, "God**

27   **speed you," but something choked the words in**

28   **my throat. He went by quickly; and "the blessing**

29   **of God on you," says he, and I could say nothing.**

30   **I looked up then, and I crying, at the gray pony,**

31   **and there was Michael upon it—with fine clothes**

32   **on him, and new shoes on his feet.**

33   **CATHLEEN:** *(Begins to keen)* **It's destroyed we are**

34   **from this day. It's destroyed, surely.**

35   **NORA:** **Didn't the young priest say that Almighty**

1   God wouldn't leave her destitute with no son

2   living?

3   MAURYA: *(In a low voice, but clearly)* It's little the

4   like of him knows of the sea. . . . Bartley will be

5   lost now, and let you call in Eamon and make

6   me a good coffin out of the white boards, for I

7   won't live after them. I've had a husband, and

8   a husband's father, and six sons in this house—

9   six fine men, though it was a hard birth I had

10   with every one of them and they coming to the

11   world—and some of them were found and some

12   of them were not found, but they're gone now

13   the lot of them. . . . There were Stephen, and

14   Shawn, were lost in the great wind, and found

15   after in the Bay of Gregory of the Golden Mouth,

16   and carried up the two of them on the one plank,

17   and in by that door. *(She pauses for a moment. The*

18   *girls start as if they heard something through the*

19   *door that is half open behind them.)*

20   NORA: *(In a whisper)* Did you hear that, Cathleen?

21   Did you hear a noise in the northeast?

22   CATHLEEN: *(In a whisper)* There's some one after

23   crying out by the seashore.

24   MAURYA: *(Continues without hearing anything.)*

25   There was Sheamus and his father, and his own

26   father again, were lost in a dark night, and not

27   a stick or sign was seen of them when the sun

28   went up. There was Patch after was drowned

29   out of a curagh that turned over. I was sitting

30   here with Bartley, and he a baby, lying on my

31   two knees, and I seen two women, and three

32   women, and four women coming in, and they

33   crossing themselves, and not saying a word. I

34   looked out then, and there were men coming

35   after them, and they holding a thing in the half

1	of a red sail, and water dripping out of it—it was
2	a dry day, Nora—and leaving a track to the door.
3	*(She pauses again with her hand stretched out toward*
4	*the door. It opens softly and old women begin to come*
5	*in, crossing themselves on the threshold, and kneeling*
6	*down in front of the stage with red petticoats over*
7	*their heads. She speaks, half in a dream, to CATH-*
8	*LEEN.)* Is it Patch or Michael, or what is it at all?
9	CATHLEEN: Michael is after being found in the Far
10	North, and when he is found there how could
11	he be here in this place?
12	MAURYA: There does be a power of young men
13	floating round in the sea, and what way would
14	they know if it was Michael they had, or another
15	man like him, for when a man is nine days in
16	the sea, and the wind blowing, it's hard set his
17	own mother would be to say what man was it.
18	CATHLEEN: It's Michael, God spare him, for
19	they're after sending us a bit of his clothes from
20	the Far North. *(She reaches out and hands*
21	*MAURYA the clothes that belonged to Michael.*
22	*MAURYA stands up slowly, and takes them in her*
23	*hands. NORA looks out.)*
24	NORA: They're carrying a thing among them and
25	there's water dripping out of it and leaving a
26	track by the big stones.
27	CATHLEEN: *(In a whisper to the women who have come*
28	*in)* Is it Bartley it is?

Planning the Blocking

Blocking means determining the placement and movement of the actors throughout the play. Some directors like to plan this out completely before rehearsing the play. Others may do little or no planning.

A director usually plans the broad movements, allowing the

actor freedom of gesture and movement within a stage area. Usually, the more experienced the actor the less direction he or she needs.

If the director plans too much ahead of time, there is a chance the action will come across as mechanical. If too little blocking is planned, there may be a great deal of time wasted figuring it out during the rehearsal periods.

Most directors include a record of the blocking in the margins of the prompt book. This is done in one of two ways. The first is by writing out the directions. The second way is by drawing sketches of the set showing where the actors are placed and how they are to move. Many directors use a combination of the two methods.

This is the case in the illustration on page 92. Notice that the sketch includes an indication of the furniture and the placement of doors. For exterior scenes, of course, the diagram would show the placement of trees, rocks and so on.

Often the director finds that what looked fine on paper does not necessarily work on the stage. So it is a good idea to use a pencil when doing the blocking. Even later in rehearsal the director or the actors may find that something about the placement or movement does not work and has to be changed.

When planning the blocking, the director has to keep several things in mind. First, it is important to present a pleasing picture at all times. Second, all the important actors in a scene have to be placed so they are in view of the audience at all times. Because of this the director has to be aware of the sightlines, that is, that nothing on the set blocks the actor from view of anyone in the audience.

In most cases, the script should determine when the broad movements occur and often exactly what they are, particularly for such things as exits and entrances. Incidentally, in most printed scripts you will see stage directions that tell where and how an actor is to move. A director may or may not follow any of these directions. They are there for one of two reasons: As a record of how the movement was planned during the play's first performance and before the script was published. Or, if the play has never been produced, they are how the playwright visualizes the action.

Often you will hear about *stage business*. There are two types, *inherent* and *supplementary*. The first refers to movement of any kind that advances or is important to the plot. Examples would be exits, entrances, answering the phone, firing a gun, and so on. Supplementary business is the kind that is added for effect.

Will crosses to the TV and turns it off

LARRY: It's impossible, totally impossible. You know *Lear* and *Julius Caesar* and *Hamlet* and *As You Like It*. You haven't been reading them, have you? While I've been at school?

WILL: Those names are not familiar.

LARRY: Of course not. And yet . . .

WILL: I swear, as long as men can breathe and eyes can see, I'll never understand your riddles. *—Turning to Larry*

LARRY: You did it again.

WILL: I didn't do anything. I was just going to say that unless you explain—

LARRY: But you did do it. Without knowing what you were doing. Shakespeare's sonnet. Number eighteen, I think. You paraphrased the next to last line. You haven't been reading the sonnets, have you?

He rushes to the window UL and looks outside.

WILL: Sonnet? What's a sonnet? I am insane! I am! Six stories up. Isn't that what we are? If I got a running start and leaped right through . . . *Facing Larry*

LARRY: Don't think such a thing. Yours is one of the greatest minds in—

WILL: Greatest minds! I don't even know who I am.

LARRY: Come and sit down. *He crosses to Will and leads him back to the sofa*

Will sits and covers his face with his hands.

WILL: To me this is a prison . . . because I cannot remember. And I despair. Yet— There is nothing either good or bad, but thinking makes it so. Isn't that right?

LARRY: *Hamlet* again. Same act. Same scene. It must be one of your favorites.

This is a page from a typical prompt book.

It helps establish the kind of person a character is and helps establish the mood of the scene and the emotions of the character. It includes the way a character stands—for instance, with drooping shoulders. It also refers to how a person moves, with jerky steps or in a regal manner, for example. This type of business includes anything the actor does to make the character clear to the audience, such as constantly relighting a pipe or twisting the ring on a finger.

The supplementary business is the type that the actor often figures out, although it can be suggested by the director.

Both types of business are used to call attention to the actor or to emphasize something important in the plot. For example, a moving actor demands more attention than one who stays in one place.

When planning the blocking, there are many other things to consider. One is placement for emphasis. For example, an important character often appears by himself or herself while others are grouped together. The important character is often placed at a higher level. This could mean the person stands while others sit, or is on a platform or landing while others are on the main floor.

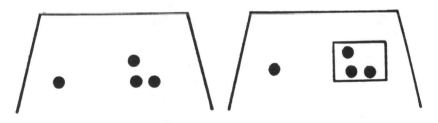

In the drawing on the left the character who stands alone draws more attention. In the drawing on the right the three actors are on a platform, drawing as much or more attention to themselves than the single actor.

It conveys strength to have an actor move directly from one place to another without circling around furniture. An exception is shown on page 94.

The actor going from Down Left to Right Center walks in a curving line. If the person did not do this, his or her back would be to the audience, which is a weak position.

Some areas of the stage are stronger, that is, they are better for emphasis. For instance, Down Center (DC) is the strongest position. This can change, however, if a group of actors are Down Center looking Up Right (UR) at an actor standing on a platform and facing them.

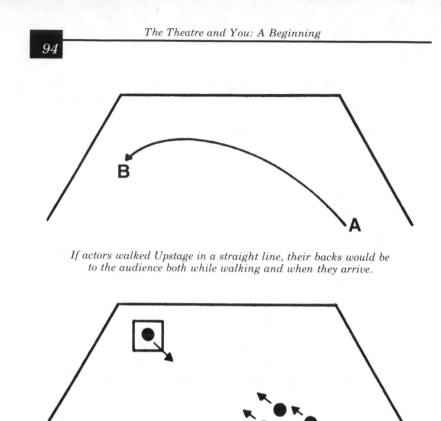

If actors walked Upstage in a straight line, their backs would be to the audience both while walking and when they arrive.

The actor Upper Right is in a much stronger position than the actors Center.

The following shows the areas of the stage from strongest to weakest, gradually decreasing in strength from the lower numbers to the higher.

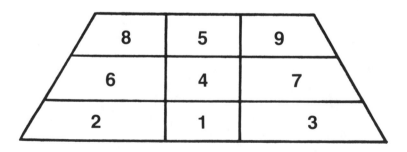

The strongest area of a stage is #1, Down Center.
The areas gradually decrease in strength as shown.

Body position also affects strength. An actor who is facing front shows the strongest position. Nearly as strong is the quarter profile, while the other positions, as shown below, decrease in strength, ending with the actor who has his back to the audience, which shouldn't be done except for a particular purpose.

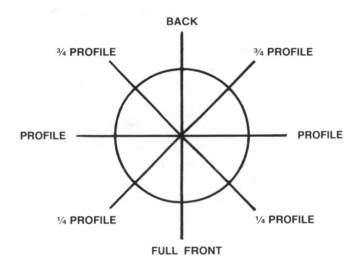

The strongest body position is full front,
the weakest with the back to the audience.

Exercises

1. Prepare a prompt book for one of the following short scenes. The easiest way is to photocopy a script, placing each page in the center of 8½- by 11-inch (typing size) paper. Include a director's analysis sheet to fill out as you go along.
2. Take the same play and figure out the central idea, the prevailing mood and the character analysis.
3. Plan the blocking for one of the following scenes. That, of course, means drawing a sketch that first shows placement of furniture and so on. Then write out in sentence form, diagram the action or use a combination of the two methods. Be as imaginative as you can.

1 # We Are, You Are, They Are
2
3 BILL: *(To the PROFESSOR)* As you know, I am Pro-
4   testant, white, and twenty-one, and my batting
5   average is 500. Therefore I feel I am qualified to
6   lead the discussion of the subject at hand.
7 SALLY: Which is . . .
8 JIM: Which is . . .
9 DOTTY: Which is . . .
10 BILL: Which is: Babies and the mystical way in
11   which they appear on the earth.
12 PROFESSOR: A very worthwhile topic. One that I
13   would expect to hear discussed only by a scholar
14   with the highest of intelligence quotients.
15 DOTTY: *(Unsure of herself)* Professor, if I may—
16 PROFESSOR: Yes, Dotty. Don't be afraid.
17 DOTTY: If you're sure it's all right.
18 BILL: We are eagerly awaiting your words, Miss
19   Dotty.
20 DOTTY: All right, then, if you insist.
21 SALLY: *(Encouragingly)* Oh, we do, don't we, class-
22   mates, and Herr professor doctor?
23 JIM: *(Speaking simultaneously with PROFESSOR)*
24   Yes.
25 PROFESSOR: *(Simultaneously with JIM)* Certainly.
26 DOTTY: All right, then. I have found through a sub-
27   tle combination of colors that the mixture of blue
28   and yellow by no means results in red.
29 PROFESSOR: Amazing! Imagine, for one so young.
30 BILL: Of course, you know, professor, that Dotty
31   next month is assuming the position of intellec-
32   tual overseer at Harvard Girls' School.
33 PROFESSOR: Oh, certainly, certainly. The thought
34   did escape my memory. However, that accounts
35   for the fact that her observation and experimen-

1   tation are so far advanced for one of her
2   chronological age.
3 DOTTY: *(Demurely)* Thank you very much, Profes-
4   sor.
5 SALLY: *(Eagerly)* I know something too.
6 PROFESSOR: And what is that, my dear young
7   lady?
8 SALLY: Blue and yellow mixed together make
9   green.
10 JIM: Oh, Sally, act your age.
11 PROFESSOR: *(Chuckling)* It is rather humorous,
12   isn't it?
13 BILL: *(To SALLY)* Why don't you ever use your
14   brain?
15 SALLY: *(Hurt)* Well, it does, doesn't it?
16 PROFESSOR: Of course, but any kindergarten
17   child knows that much. Now if you had the in-
18   quisitive intellect of that of the other feminine
19   member of this class— Humph! But you with
20   your kindergarten education presume to tell the
21   rest of us, who have such obviously superior
22   thinking mechanisms, a simple truth such as
23   that, why you are completely wasting your time
24   and ours.
25 SALLY: *(Almost crying)* Red and yellow make
26   orange.
27 PROFESSOR: Tut, tut, my child.
28 BILL: Oh, brother.
29 JIM: *(Angrily)* I'm not your brother.
30 DOTTY: There, there, Sally. It's all right.
31 SALLY: Red and white make pink. *(The others show*
32   *an actual physical aversion to SALLY.)* Blue and
33   red make magenta. *(She begins to cry.)* Black and
34   white make grey. Blue and black, make blue-
35   black, red and yellow and gold and brown make

1   red-yellow-gold-brown.

2   PROFESSOR: Young lady, I suggest you go to the

3   powder room and powder your nose. *(SALLY*

4   *rushes from the room.)* **Well, class, you have wit-**

5   nessed one of the saddest spectacles possible—

6   the deterioration of a human intellect.

7   JIM: It's spreading like a disease.

8   PROFESSOR: It certainly is shocking, but there ap-

9   pears to be no recourse.

10

11

The Tattoo Parlor

by Louis Phillips

15   *(There is the sound of a car pulling up, a door closing.*

16   *A woman appears in the doorway. An apparition.*

17   *Almost. She is DARLENE META, 20 to 21 years old,*

18   *dressed in a very proper skirt-and-blouse combina-*

19   *tion; she is definitely out of her element.)*

20   DARLENE: Is this really a tattoo parlor? *(CARLE-*

21   *TON is too stunned to reply.)* **Yoo-hoo.**

22   CARLETON: You talking to me, lady?

23   DARLENE: Is this where people come to get tat-

24   tooed?

25   CARLETON: I guess so. I know they don't come

26   here to buy groceries.

27   DARLENE: Good. Stay where you are and I'll be

28   right back. . . . I just have to pay the cab-

29   driver. . . . Don't go away.

30   CARLETON: Wait a minute, lady! *(Too late. The ap-*

31   *parition has vanished.)* **I'm not open for business**

32   now. I just had the door open so I could listen

33   to the rain. *(DARLENE returns carrying a small*

34   *green suitcase and an umbrella. We hear the cab driv-*

35   *ing off.)* **I wouldn't let that cab go if I were you.**

1   DARLENE: Why not?

2   CARLETON: Because . . . Oh, forget it. *(In the light*

3   *we can see that DARLENE has been crying, her eyes*

4   *are slightly puffy.)*

5   DARLENE: Can I put my suitcase down?

6   CARLETON: As long as you're not planning to

7   move in.

8   DARLENE: You don't know how glad I am to find

9   a place like this. I've been looking all over for

10   a tattoo parlor, and the cab driver remembered

11   that there was one down by the docks.

12   CARLETON: You're not a lawyer by any chance?

13   DARLENE: I'm going to be an architect.

14   CARLETON: Oh.

15   DARLENE: Why?

16   CARLETON: Because as soon as somebody says

17   that they've been looking all over for me, I know

18   it means trouble. *(CARLETON closes the door.)*

19   DARLENE: Why did you close the door?

20   CARLETON: There are not too many things to do

21   with a door. You open it. You close it. I usually

22   close it when I have a client. What's the matter?

23   You frightened?

24   DARLENE: *(Frightened)* No. I'm not frightened.

25   Your place just seems different with the door

26   closed.

27   CARLETON: You should have seen it before the

28   roof was put on. Look, if it'll make you feel any

29   better, I'll keep the door open. *(He opens the door.)*

30   But if anybody sees somebody like you in here,

31   they'll just come walking right in, and some of

32   them are pretty rough. All I guarantee is the

33   permanence of the tattoo. I can't guarantee the

34   personal safety of my customers. I used to have

35   a sign that said it, but it's been torn down.

1   DARLENE: You're right. Perhaps you'd better
2   keep it closed.
3   CARLETON: *(Closing the door)* I don't care which.
4   Just make up your mind. After all, I didn't invite
5   you here.
6   DARLENE: You didn't seem to be afraid of people
7   walking in on you.
8   CARLETON: If I were in a different line of business,
9   I'd be afraid, but, as it is, nobody steals tat-
10   toos. . . . Want a beer?
11 DARLENE: No, thank you. It took me three drinks
12   to get here. . . . Pink ladies.
13 CARLETON: How about some tea. I'll put some tea
14   on.
15 DARLENE: Tea?
16 CARLETON: Yeah, you know. Tea . . . Help dry you
17   out.
18 DARLENE: Oh no. You're not going to drug me and
19   sell me to some white slave trader. Just give me
20   my tattoos and I'll go home.
21 CARLETON: Just give you your tattoos and you'll
22   go home. What do you think I do, lady? Just put
23   it in a paper-sack like a chicken salad sandwich?
24   Tattooing isn't done like that.
25 DARLENE: Why must everything be so compli-
26   cated? When my brother and I were growing up,
27   we'd buy these pictures for a penny, spit on
28   them, and rub them right on to our skin.
29 CARLETON: If you want something like that, you
30   go to a dime store, not a tattoo parlor.
31 DARLENE: You call this a parlor.
32 CARLETON: I wasn't planning on entertaining
33   Queen Victoria tonight.
34 DARLENE: There's no need to take that tone with
35   me.

1   CARLETON: Well, we don't spit on our tattoos
2   around here. *(He finds a glass, spits into it to clean*
3   *it for the tea, wipes it out with his shirt.)*
4   DARLENE: I think I'll pass up the tea.
5   CARLETON: Pass up the tattooing while you're at
6   it.
7   DARLENE: Oh, no. You're not going to talk me out
8   of it. I know what I want. I want to be made
9   exotic. No man is ever going to call me dull and
10   uninteresting again. I'll show him.
11 CARLETON: Is that why you've been crying? Be-
12   cause some man said you were uninteresting?
13 DARLENE: Do you think I've been crying?
14 CARLETON: You look like you've been crying.
15 DARLENE: Are my eyes all puffy? I hate it when
16   my eyes get all puffy.
17 CARLETON: What's your name?
18 DARLENE: There's no need to get intimate. I just
19   want a tattoo.
20 CARLETON: I just asked.
21 DARLENE: If I wanted counseling, I could have
22   gone to the YWCA.
23 CARLETON: You certainly would have been better
24   off there than running around deserted docks
25   at two o'clock in the morning.
26 DARLENE: My name is Darlene and it's not two
27   o'clock in the morning. *(CARLETON pulls out a*
28   *silver pocket watch and snaps it open.)*
29 CARLETON: Not in Hawaii, it's not. But here it's
30   1:47 . . . But then Boston has always been a bit
31   behind the rest of the world.
32 DARLENE: I didn't realize it was that late.
33 CARLETON: If you missed it the first time, it'll come
34   around again.

CHAPTER SEVEN
Casting and Rehearsing

After a director has finished the planning, the next step is to cast the show and start rehearsals.

Casting the Play

Even though a director has thought through the ideas for a play, he or she has to keep an open mind when choosing a cast, or it will be hard to find actors to fit the parts.

Auditions

Well-known professional director Harold Clurman once said that the way to be a good director is to choose a good script and then choose good actors.

There are two general types of auditions, *open tryouts* and *interviews*. The first is the most common.

In professional theatre the open tryout is sometimes referred to as the "cattle call." This is because everyone comes to the theatre (or rehearsal space) at the same time and auditions in front of everyone else.

There are variations on how this is done. Most often the director will have the actors give a *cold reading*. This means the director chooses a passage in the play and has the actors read it without having much of a chance to go over it.

Sometimes, however, directors will allow those who want to audition to sign out a script overnight so they can become familiar with the play. In some cases, directors will simply assign the actor to read a particular part during auditions. At other times, they will ask those auditioning if there is any role for which they particularly want to read. Even then a director will often have them read another role he or she thinks they may fit better.

The open tryout has several advantages. First it shows how different actors work and look together. Often two people who appear in the same scene will provide a spark that isn't there when they work with anyone else. Also, it shows how the actors appear together physically. In that way, there is little danger of casting a husband who is five inches shorter than his wife.

Another advantage is that the director can better compare those who audition for a particular role because they appear at the same general time.

A disadvantage is that actors often are affected by the way others audition. Some may lose confidence because they feel they are not doing as well as the others. A second disadvantage is that if the auditions run for a long time the director may have trouble concentrating, which is not fair to the actors who read during the latter part of the rehearsal.

Sometimes the director will tell the actors to improvise (make up the action and dialog) a scene, rather than reading from the script.

For the interview method, each actor appears individually. The director may simply talk to the actor and ask questions about background, experience and so on. This is to get an idea of how well the person handles himself or herself in front of others.

Sometimes in the interview audition the director will have the actor read a particular part while the director reads the other parts. The advantage is that the director can concentrate just on one person, rather than two or three actors who are reading a scene. At the same time this is a disadvantage in that the director also is reading and cannot give full attention to the actor's physical reactions.

Just as in open tryouts, the director may ask the actor to improvise a scene. Here, of course, it would be a monolog.

In professional theatre, experienced actors often are interviewed while those with less experience or auditioning for minor roles go to open tryouts.

No matter which type of audition the director favors, he or she has a variety of things to consider. They include how well the actors move, how much emotional depth they bring to the audition, the quality, range and projection of their voices and their overall potential for a role.

Often actors will need special abilities, like being able to sing or dance. Then the director often has them come with a prepared song and maybe a prepared dance, although they may be asked to memorize a few steps and then perform them at the audition.

Often there will be callbacks where the director has narrowed the choices down to a few for each role. Because there are fewer people the director can concentrate more on each person.

During the auditions, a director has to be able to keep track of which person is which. Professionals usually have an actor's resumé, which lists training and experience and includes a photo. Often directors in nonprofessional theatre will have the actors fill out a sheet that tells about their background. Sometimes the director will take a Polaroid shot of each actor.

Throughout the auditions the director makes notes about how each person did.

Finally, out of all this the director chooses the cast and begins rehearsals.

Exercises

1. Choose a scene from anywhere in the book—maybe the scene you have already blocked—and make a list of the sort of things you are looking for in each role. Share what you have done with the rest of the class. If any of you have chosen the same scene or play, how do your ideas differ? If you are unhappy with the scene you originally chose, pick a new one. You will be working with it for a number of exercises.

2. With the same scene hold auditions, using whatever method you wish. You can use other members of your class or people from outside the class. Have your classmates critique the way you handled things. They should tell you both what they liked and what they think could be improved.

3. Now choose your cast and be able to explain why you chose each person.

Rehearsing the Play

In nonprofessional theatre the rehearsal period is usually six weeks for a straight play and eight weeks for a musical. In professional theatre the period is usually a couple of weeks less. This is because professional actors can spend all day rehearsing.

There are six stages of rehearsal. They are *reading rehearsals, blocking rehearsals, character and line rehearsals, finishing rehearsals, technical rehearsals* and *dress rehearsals.*

The length for each type depends on a lot of things. One is the background and experience of the actors. In educational theatre the director often is a teacher as well because the actors, with little or no experience, haven't ever had a chance to learn what is expected of them, so they need a longer rehearsal period.

Some plays simply are easier to perform than others. For instance, it usually takes a shorter time to prepare a modern melodrama than a Greek tragedy.

This actor is reading for the director at an open audition.

There is no set time for each type of rehearsal either. When the business and blocking are complicated, the blocking rehearsals will be longer.

Character and line rehearsals take longer if the lines are difficult and the characters involved. For example, it probably would take a lot longer to learn and deliver Shakespeare's lines than it would to learn and deliver the lines in many modern plays.

Also, if the play has a lot of special effects, the technical rehearsals will be longer.

Reading Rehearsals

The purpose of reading rehearsals is to come to a clear understanding and interpretation of the play so everyone will know what is expected of them. For instance, the director may see a comedy as subtle, while one of the actors may have decided on a broad style of acting, using exaggerated gestures and movement and exaggerated vocal qualities.

Although some directors have an exact idea of how they want the play interpreted, others are willing to listen to actors' suggestions. If what the actors say seems appropriate, the director may change his or her own ideas. Or the director may disagree and ask the actors to try to interpret their roles a different way.

The director often discusses the theme and the subject matter of the play and their importance. There is a thorough discussion of the play as a whole, including the goals and needs of each character. The actors need to understand the place of their characters in the overall story, as well as the story itself.

Often reading rehearsals aren't held on stage, but in a room where everyone can sit and discuss the play.

Sometimes the director will ask the actors to read the play aloud to get an overall feeling for it without worrying about interpreting their characters. At some point the director may show sketches and floor plans of the scene design to the actors so they can see what the set will be like.

The reading rehearsal usually lasts two to four days to make sure everyone is on the right track in their interpretation.

Exercises

1. Take a few days to do this exercise in class, allowing 10 to 15 minutes for each director. With the rest of the

class observing what you do, discuss the play with the cast you have already chosen. Tell them how you interpret it, what it means and how you think it should be presented. Allow the actors to offer ideas and suggestions.

2. After each person does exercise one, have the class discuss how the director handled the assignment. What did the class like about each rehearsal? What could be improved?

Blocking Rehearsals

During blocking rehearsals the physical actions, movement and business are worked out. These are important not only because the script requires that certain things be done but also to give the play life. The director also has to be aware of sightlines and if the actors can be seen from all parts of the auditorium.

The director uses movement and placement to emphasize what is important at every point in the play. The movement should grow out of the script.

It takes a great deal of thought to block a play since the blocking has to fit not only the action and plot but the type of play. Actors in a tragedy probably would move and even speak more slowly than in a fast-paced comedy. Comedy would be deadly presented in a slow, deliberate manner.

Although the movement is planned just after the reading rehearsals, it continues to build and change throughout the rehearsal period. In many cases, the director will want to change things later on. This is why actors should always carry pencils to mark down where and how they are to move.

Exercises

1. Using the scene you blocked on paper, instruct your cast about placement and movement. Because this takes a long time to do, just go through a page or two in front of the rest of the class.

2. After you have blocked the one or two pages, run through it one or two times and change anything you don't like. Your actors should suggest whatever they think can be changed to improve the scene. But remember that you have the final say.

This actor is being directed where to move in the musical, Sugar.

3.   Have the rest of the class critique what you've done.
4.   If possible, outside of class or after school, go through the rest of the scene in the same way. Have your actors start memorizing their lines.

Character and Line Rehearsal

During the script analysis the actors begin working on interpretation. But it is after the blocking rehearsals, which are probably the most mechanical of all six types, that they begin to concentrate fully on building and developing the roles they will play. This is when each of the characters really starts to come to life.

Sometimes a director still will pull an actor aside and say that the interpretation isn't working or doesn't fit with the overall concept. Now the actors work on the interpretations of each line of dialog, as well as their overall character.

Line and character interpretation go hand in hand. Once a character is established, the person has a distinctive way of speaking that applies to all the lines.

During character and line rehearsals the director makes sure the actors understand the significance and importance of each of their lines. That is not to say that all lines are equally important. Some are "throw-away" lines, casual hellos and good-byes, for instance.

As part of the prompt book, directors usually underline or highlight with a marking pen all the lines that are particularly important to the action and the advancement of the plot. This is so the actor delivering them will be the center of focus and can deliver the lines clearly.

During these rehearsals directors also pay attention to how well the actors are doing technically in projecting both their lines and their characters.

Exercises

1. Direct the actors in your scene to interpret and build their characters, paying attention to and reacting in character to the other actors in the scene. Go through the scene several times—outside of class, if possible— and then present it to the rest of the class.

2. Make notes during the final running of the scene, which should be in front of the class. Now, using the notes, tell the actors what they did well and what they need to improve.

3. Have the rest of the class discuss with you what you have done and why you have done it in that particular way.

Finishing Rehearsals

During this period the actors' performances are polished and "finished." That is, the interpretations should be pretty well set and the characters and line delivery established. Up to this time the director has stopped scenes when necessary to correct blocking or line delivery and interpretation. From now on, unless something is seriously wrong, the director goes through each act without stopping. This way everyone gets a better idea of how everything is working. Throughout the running of each act, the director takes notes and later goes over them with the actors.

Throughout the earlier rehearsals and the first finishing rehearsals, the director has the actors go through only one act or several scenes during each rehearsal. It would be too difficult to try to put the entire play together and rehearse the whole thing during every rehearsal period. In fact, during the blocking rehearsals it may take several hours to get through eight or 10 pages.

Before the end of the finishing rehearsals, there will be *run-throughs* of the entire play, stopping only between acts for notes.

Until the run-throughs begin, it is difficult to pay attention to the show's overall movement because there have been too many stops. Now directors begin to concentrate on three broad aspects of the play's movement. They are *pace, timing* and *rhythm.*

Pace is the fastness or slowness overall in handling lines and business. It is always faster in tense or exciting scenes and slower in a relaxed mood. All plays, even tragedies which always are slower than comedies, will become boring and tedious if they drag. Similarly, they will be hard to follow if the pace is too fast.

Timing means the pauses between or within speeches. Maybe the best way to think of this is to think of a comedian you saw on TV. If the person was funny, no doubt a large part of the reason is his or her sense of timing. A pause points up or emphasizes what is to follow, like the punchline of a joke. Yet if it's too long, the punchline won't seem funny.

In both comic and serious plays, the timing of reactions is important. For example, one character tells another that something bad has happened. The second character pauses in shock for a moment before answering. Pauses are just as important as the lines themselves.

Rhythm refers to the flow of the lines and includes how quickly actors pick up on their cue lines, those lines directly preceding each speech. Every play, mainly because of the style in which it is written, has a certain rhythm.

Exercises

1.   Work with your actors on the three aspects of move-

ment. Again, if possible, rehearse the scene several times outside of class. For the final finishing rehearsal, present the scene to the class.

2.   Using your notes, talk to the actors about how well they have done and what they could do better.

3.   Have the actors tell you how well they think the scene went and why. Then let the rest of the class question you on what you wanted to achieve with the scene and how well this came across.

Technical Rehearsals

By the time the technical rehearsals start, the acting should be pretty much as it will be during the performance. It is now that all attention is on such things as lighting and the shifting of scenery and properties. The director will now be paying attention to these things rather than to the actors' performances.

If everything has been well planned there should be little problem and things should run smoothly. Often at this point the stage manager takes care of the run-throughs, seeing that all aspects of the show run smoothly.

Dress Rehearsals

The dress rehearsal is the tryout period for a show, much in the same way that plays bound for Broadway are often presented in other theatres first.

As a matter of fact, some directors prefer to have invited audiences at dress rehearsals so the performers can learn to react to people in the auditorium.

Most often there are two rehearsals in full costume with all the technical aspects of the show. These rehearsals should run exactly like performances. From here on the director's only responsibility is to take notes during performance and give them to the actors some time before the next showing.

If the play is to have a long run, the director may call rehearsals occasionally to correct anything that is inconsistent with what was originally planned.

Exercises

1. Now that the scene is done with, what would you change about it if you could? What would you have done differently? Make a few notes on this and, if your teacher calls on you, tell the rest of the class what you have discovered as a result of directing this scene.

2. If possible, go see a play with the rest of the class and take notes on what you like and what you dislike about the way it was directed. Compare your ideas with those of your classmates.

3. At this point discuss with the rest of the class what you like and dislike about being a director. Is this something you would like to continue? Why or why not?

Directing in Arena Theatre

Body position does not mean much in arena theatre because an actor who is open to one area of the audience has his back to another part. Spacing also is not too important because an actor who appears to be separated from the group at one angle will appear closer to the other actors from another angle.

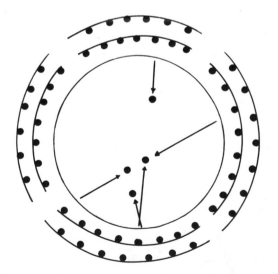

The arrows show that certain audience members probably wouldn't be able to see one of the actors or at least would have difficulty telling how much space there is between the actors in their direct line of sight.

Instead body positions relate to other actors and not to the audience. To show emotional closeness or distancing an actor can move toward or away from another actor. For the most part, movement is rarely in a direct line. By moving in a curved line the actor is open to more parts of the audience.

Usually, if actors keep at least four or five feet of space between each other, the scenes will be opened for all of the audience. If two actors are facing each other directly at close range, all that most of the audience sees is their backs since each blocks the other's face. So it is better if each stands slightly sideways in relation to the other.

Most positions are all right if they are held only for a short time. Even minor or subtle movements give the audience the impression of having a better view. In two-character scenes, the director can place one or both actors near an aisleway, providing better sightlines. Often, because the actor who is speaking cannot be the center of attention for the entire audience, reactions and facial expressions become more important.

In arena theatre it is easier to block three characters because there can then be a triangle, opening two actors out of the three to every part of the house, but only if they are not near an aisleway.

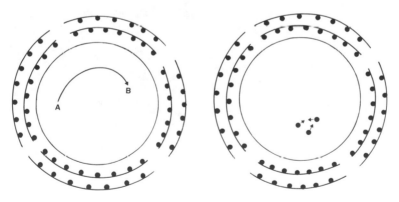

Moving in a curved line rather than a straight one, as illustrated at left, is better in arena theatre. A triangle (unless the actors are very close physically) allows all members of the audience to see at least part of the faces of two of the actors in an arena theatre, as shown at right.

The tempo of a play in arena theatre is usually faster because the lines and characters do not have to be projected so far. The movements can be more subtle, the dialog closer to a conversational tone. Of course, this depends on the size of the audience part. The larger the audience area, the less subtle the acting can be.

Exercises

1. Take the same scene and the same actors you used earlier in the chapter and block the play for arena theatre. At first you may have to keep moving around the stage area to judge how the placement and movement look. Later you can probably begin to visualize it without actually moving.
2. How does arena theatre change what you have to do to have your scene come across well?
3. Have the class critique what you have done.
4. Which type of theatre do you prefer for directing: Proscenium or arena? Why?

PART III
DESIGN

CHAPTER EIGHT
Scenery and Lighting

All the designers work with each other to bring life visually to the director's ideas.

The designers meet together, often trading sketches and ideas that go along with what the director wants. Often the designers will inspire the director to create something beyond what he or she first visualized.

The Scene Designer

One of the people important in bringing the play to life is the scene designer whose work is similar to that of an architect, though not as permanent because as soon as a production's run is finished the set is *struck* (dismantled).

The Functions of Scene Design

First, as you learned, the setting provides either an environ ment or a background for the playwright's ideas. It can help convey the theme and provides information that helps the audience understand the play. For example, it shows the location and often the financial circumstances and tastes of the characters.

In addition the set helps set the mood. If, for instance, it uses bright colors and the feeling of openness, the audience will surmise that the play is lighthearted. On the other hand, lots of dark colors and imposing set pieces would convey a somber or serious feeling.

The setting, similar to a lighted TV or movie screen, provides a focal point for the audience. Also, the stage may be divided into areas that represent different rooms in a house. Each area is a focal point at different times during the play. This is done partly in collaboration with the lighting designer who further isolates each area and points out which part of the setting should draw the audience's attention at any particular time.

As you learned, every part of the setting should be easily seen from every part of the auditorium.

Another consideration is that the set should be easy for the actors to use. If they have difficulty coming down a stairway because the treads are too narrow, this takes too much of the actor's attention which should be focused on line delivery and character interpretation. This is why the treads on stage stairs often are a little wider than those in a house. On the other hand, they are the same height as regular steps, or the actors would have to concentrate on not stumbling.

Even though the set will be struck when the production is finished, it has to be well constructed. A staircase or a platform has to support the actors. Windows and doors, if they are to be used by the actor, must open and close easily. If they don't, the audience will begin paying attention to them instead of to the progression of the play. Much of this, of course, depends on the way the stage carpenter and his crew have constructed the set pieces. But the designer has to know when and how to brace the legs of a platform.

The setting also has to present a picture that is pleasing. This doesn't mean it has to be beautiful. It means that it has to be accurate in showing the location or the action. Like everything else in the production, the setting should not stand out or call attention to itself to the extent that it overshadows all the other elements.

The setting, through color and shape, helps communicate the style and genre of a play.

For instance, the setting for A Thurber Carnival prepares the audience for something light because of the colors and also something presentational, that is, suggestive of life rather than representing it. An audience should be able to tell immediately whether a set is supposed to be realistic or nonrealistic. If nonrealistic, the shapes and colors should help create the proper mood.

Curved lines and shapes suggest lightness or playfulness whereas straight or angular shapes suggest somberness or seriousness.

The designer can exaggerate elements of the setting to suggest certain qualities. For example, because the characters in a farce are two-dimensional, the set pieces are often cutouts.

Exercises

1. Take the scene you have been working with or another scene from the book and write a description of the sort of set you would like. How and what should it communicate to an audience?
2. Using the same scene, what would you include in the setting to help convey the mood and theme of the play? Discuss this with the rest of the class.

Balance and Harmony

A stage setting should be balanced. This can either be symmetrically or asymmetrically. *Symmetrical balance* means that the left half of the set contains exactly the same elements as the right half. This is the kind of balance the human body has if you imagine a straight line right down the middle.

Symmetrical balance is rarely used except for classical Greek plays where no specific location is represented. The sense of place is suggested rather than indicated.

More common is *asymmetrical balance*, which means that although the elements on each side of the stage are not the same, they have the same total weight or mass so that there is a feeling of balance.

Imagine for instance the kind of scale where one side matches the other. Like this:

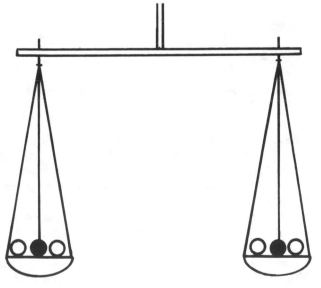

Symmetrical balance means one side is exactly like the other.

Now imagine that stones of one shape and color are placed in one side and stones of a different shape, size and color are placed in the other side. If the weight is the same, they balance, as shown in the illustration on the following page. Remember though that some colors are heavier than others. At the extreme end, black appears much heavier than white. The lighter the color, the lighter an object generally appears in weight.

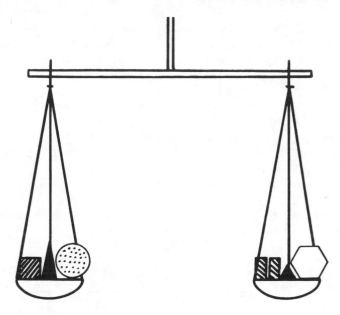

*Asymmetrical balance means unlike objects still
can be balanced through the use of weight and color.*

On the next page are a couple of examples of asymmetrical settings. The first has no furniture and does not use flats because it is for a play, *A Thurber Carnival*, which has a lot of different scenes and locations. Therefore the setting suggests place rather than portrays it.

In addition to balance, a set should have a sense of *harmony*. This means that each part of the set should look as if it really belongs or is consistent.

There can be a lot of different elements as in the play *You Can't Take It With You* where there are people with many different interests living in one dwelling. Yet all these different things support the theme of nonconformity or being an individual which is what the play is about.

On the other hand, you couldn't have part of the set for *A Thurber Carnival* look like an actual place—a garden or an office for instance, even though some scenes are supposed to occur in these sorts of places.

The designer has to have a feeling for style and be able to recognize what styles can be mingled effectively.

The set for A Thurber Carnival, *shown at top, suggests place
rather than portraying it. The set below portrays an actual place.*

Exercises

1. Which would work better for your scene, a symmetrical or an asymmetrical set? What makes you think so? What elements of setting do you actually need? Should they be realistic or would it be better just to suggest them?
2. Find someone else in class who has chosen the same scene but has different ideas about the setting. Get together and try to decide which setting is better and why. Maybe it would work to combine elements of the other person's setting and elements of yours. Tell the rest of the class why you came up with the ideas you did and what the two of you finally decided.

The Scene Designer's Background

Designers should have a sense of the artistic. Their training should consist of a lot of different things. Many set designers also design the lighting for a production. But even if they don't, they need to learn about the elements of lighting and how stage lighting works.

Scene designers need to know color theory—what colors complement each other—and the psychology of color, or what moods and feelings different colors suggest. For this, art classes help.

Since they have to be able to give accurate instructions to those who will build the sets, the designers need a background and possibly classes in draftsmanship. Knowing about architecture also is a help.

Scene designers need to be familiar with all the other areas of design, including make-up and costuming, so all the designs can mesh effectively. They should know a little about acting and directing so they can design sets that the actors can use easily and effectively. They need to understand carpentry and how sets are built so their designs can be carried out. They need to know the type of materials generally used in constructing sets and what type is best for any particular effect, as well as the costs of these materials so they can design sets that stay within the theatre's budget.

Designers have to know interior decorating. Once they design a set, they should be able to visualize what type of furniture is suitable and how it will enhance or change the set's appearance.

Because of this they have to know current styles for contemporary plays and period styles and architecture for historical plays.

Designers need to know how to use space, line, color, texture and ornamentation to build an atmosphere and environment that are fitting and workable.

Planning a Setting

Just like the director, the scene designer begins with a study and analysis of the script. But the designer's analysis is different in some ways. Although designers may start by trying to determine the mood and theme, they then spend much more time on the play's environment.

They consider where the play takes place, the time period and specifics about the setting that are either necessary to establish mood or are actually used. For instance, how many doorways or entryways are needed? Where do they lead? Can anything be seen beyond the doors—such as a lawn, trees, a garden or a hallway.

Will platforms or stairs be needed? If there are to be windows, do they need to open and close? If so, they require more work to build.

After all this, the designers think about what would look good for the particular play, making sketches as they go through the script. Although some of theses sketches may eventually be discarded, they help the designers to envision the staging requirements of the play. When they do come up with something they think will work, they meet with the director to show sketches and drawings. Maybe they have already talked with the director. Maybe not.

The drawings on the following page are not on an exact scale but merely sketches. The furniture can be cutouts to be moved around so the designer can get a good idea of what position seems to be workable. The design was for the play *Any Wednesday*, presented on the floor of a gymnasium. It is a kind of thrust stage with the audience seated on three sides.

Throughout all of the planning the scene designer meets with the other designers. Then when ideas are agreed upon, the designer prepares a more exact plan for building the set. This is called a *floor plan*, a drawing of the setting as seen from above.

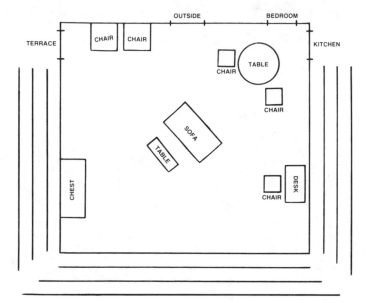

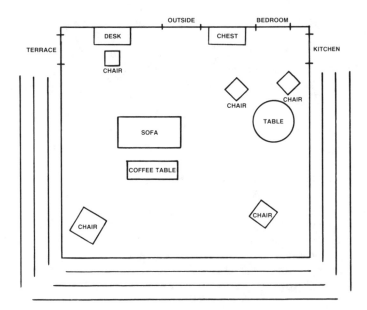

Examples of scene sketches.

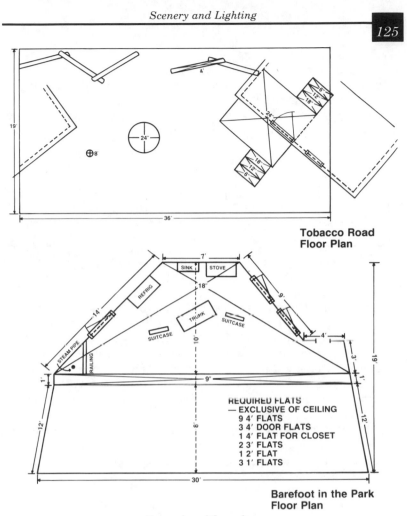

**Tobacco Road
Floor Plan**

REQUIRED FLATS
— EXCLUSIVE OF CEILING
9 4' FLATS
3 4' DOOR FLATS
1 4' FLAT FOR CLOSET
2 3' FLATS
1 2' FLAT
3 1' FLATS

**Barefoot in the Park
Floor Plan**

Examples of floor plans.

Notice in the set for *Barefoot in the Park* that there is little furniture, only what does not need to be moved in by new tenants. Later other things are moved in. The back part of the stage appears squeezed together to suggest a tiny kitchen, which is on an 18-inch-high platform to separate it from the downstage area which later will become the living room. Upstage Left is an opening that is an entryway rather than a doorway. Behind it is a four-foot flat that would be painted black simply to block the backstage area.

This shows how the set fits the stage. Sometimes designers will make several floor plans showing shifts in scenery or furniture. Sometimes they will construct a model of the set, so the director can see what it will be like and how the actors can be positioned and moved. This not only shows the shapes and types of construction but colors as well.

Both the floor plans and the model usually are done with ¼ inch (occasionally ½ inch) equalling one foot.

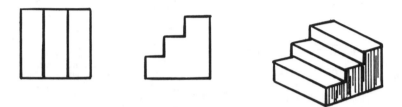

Next the designer may show steps and other three-dimensional shapes from different angles. Sometimes there are sectional views of three-dimensional objects. For instance, a drawing may show a stage rock cut open to reveal how the framework is built, covered with chicken wire first and then papier mâché. Next, if necessary, are views of an object from the corner and slightly above to give those who will construct the set a clearer understanding of platforms or figures.

The designers give copies of all the drawings to the director, the technical director (the person who supervises all the stage crews), the stage manager and the stage carpenter or whoever is to head the construction crew.

Often the designer chooses the type and style of furniture and the set dressings, although this may be the job of the *property master* (the person in charge of building or gathering all the properties). In some theatres the set designer also supervises the painting. In educational and community theatre the designer often supervises or carries out much of the construction.

Exercises

1. Do not worry about whether you draw well or not, but try to come up with sketches that show how your setting will look. Now using either paints or crayons, show the colors you would use.

2. Do a floor plan of the setting for your scene. For any three-dimensional objects, indicate the height by draw-

ing an X across the unit and printing the number of inches. For example, in the setting for *Tobacco Road* you can see that the steps that lead up to the house (you see only the porch and front wall) are six inches, 12 inches and 18 inches high. The tree is eight feet and the rail fence is four feet.

3. Do a model of your set, keeping in mind that flats come in standard sizes of usually four feet, three feet, two feet and occasionally one foot. To find out the size of doorways, simply measure some in your home or at school. Build models of any set pieces like the tree in *Tobacco Road*. Often you can find furniture in a toy department that is on a scale of ¼ or ½ inch to the foot.

4. Now pretend your scene is to be given in an arena or thrust-stage theatre and design a different setting. Remember that most of what you will use is furniture and maybe carpeting. If you design the scene for a thrust stage, of course, you can have one wall of scenery. Notice in the sketch for *Any Wednesday*, there are two exits indicated. These are imaginary and actually lead to aisleways and doors on either side of the real gymnasium wall. They lead to the locker rooms.

The Lighting Designer

Rather than simply providing illumination, the lighting of a set helps convey the mood and theme, and, of course, with blackouts, conceals scenery shifts and signals the end of an act or scene.

There are two types of stage lighting, general and specific. General lighting is largely for illumination or for having a well-lighted playing area. Specific lighting is for particular effects. It helps establish mood and helps communicate the playwright's theme through color and intensity. A dimly lighted stage, for example, can suggest something scary or mysterious, while a brightly lighted stage suggests a "lighter" mood. On the other hand, too much intensity or glaring lights can make the audience uncomfortable. Sometimes this is deliberate to suggest terrible situations as when a character is being unjustly punished or perhaps tortured.

The Functions of Lighting

Lighting can give information to the audience. It can suggest sunlight or moonlight. It can suggest nighttime through the use of floor and table lamps or sparkling chandeliers.

Lighting provides selective visibility by pointing up the important areas of the set for any particular scene. Suppose, for instance, a character leaves the living room and goes to an outside porch. The lights dim or fade to black inside and come up outside, indicating which area the audience should watch. In musicals, in particular, large spotlights often are used to focus on the major character.

Like scenery, lighting is only a symbol for something else. Just as the flats stand for walls, stage lighting stands for other things. Even a regular floor lamp on stage will not provide enough illumination. So the light of the lamp is intensified or added to, usually with lighting instruments hanging from battens overhead.

Another function of lighting is to make objects look realistic. For example, under lights, certain fabrics look much richer or more expensive than they really are. Stage rocks with proper lighting can look like the real thing.

The Lighting Designer's Background

Lighting designers should be acquainted with all areas of theatre. In addition, they certainly should be acquainted with the principles of electricity. Many lighting designers are licensed electricians.

Lighting Components

Lighting requires two separate components, the instruments that illuminate the stage and a way of controlling these instruments.

There are two major types of instruments, *floodlights* and *spotlights*. There are various types in each of these categories.

Floodlights cannot be focused and have no lens. Spotlights, which can be focused on a particular area without spilling over into other areas usually do have a lens.

Spotlights or spots come in a lot of different sizes and can focus on a very small area or a very large one. Most have a metal frame into which *gelatins*, usually called gels, can fit. These are color transparencies which usually are used to suggest or convey a mood. Green transparencies, for instance, are not used much because they provide an eerie quality. Oranges and yellows and

This is a floodlight.

reds can suggest warmth.

This is another kind of symbolism, which often depends on the play. Red, for instance, can suggest such things as passion, shame, heat and so on. The colors in themselves mean little. It is only when they are used for various scenes that they have specific meaning.

One of the most common spots is called a *Fresnel*, which illuminates an area in the shape of an oval or circle.

The lens that covers the bulb (in theatre this is called the lamp) softens the light around the edges so that it is difficult to see exactly where the lighted area ends.

The other most common spot is the *ellipsoidal reflector*. This instrument is both brighter and more controllable than a Fresnel. It has a framing device which exactly defines the lighted area.

The edge, unlike that of the Fresnel, stops abruptly. The ellipse, as it is often called, can provide a complete contrast from strong illumination to complete darkness with no light at all spilling over into the dark area.

Ellipsoidal reflectors can be used at nearly any distance from the stage, while Fresnels are almost always within 40 feet of the area to be lighted.

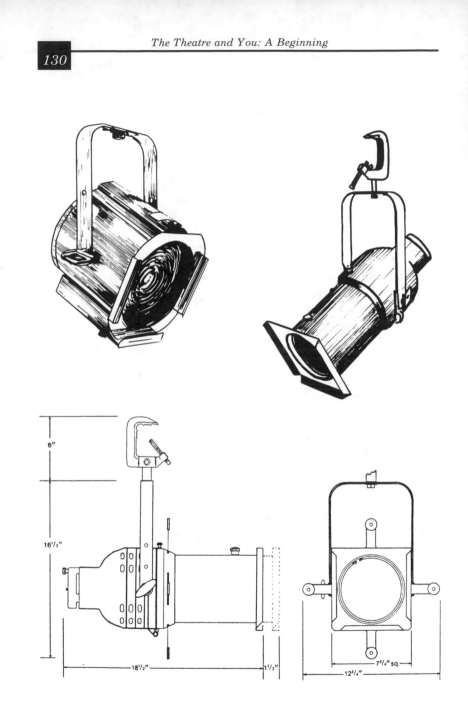

At top left is shown a Fresnel, at top right an ellipsoidal reflector. The drawings below show an ellipsoidal reflector and its framing device. The handles on the top, bottom and sides operate shutters which can be used to frame the area to be lighted.

Another common type of illumination is the *striplight*. This is a long instrument that resembles a trough. The lights in the trough are covered with colored lenses that consist of the primary colors, like this:

Striplights are often used to light the cyclorama, the curtain that hangs in a semicircle running along the sides and back of the stage.

The system that controls the lighting is the board from which someone runs the lights, that is, turning them on and off, dimming them and so on. Below is an example of a lighting board.

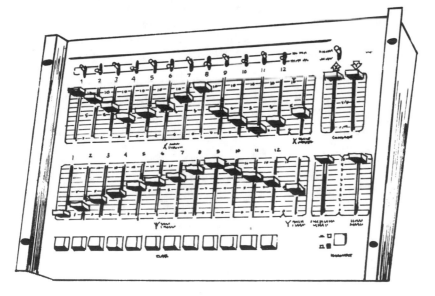

Planning the Lighting

Lighting designers analyze the script to make note of the source of light for each scene. Then they plan how to help indicate time, place and season. At the same time they try to design lighting that doesn't call attention to itself.

They have to figure out where to hang lights for the best

effect. They realize, for example, that an actor or a set piece should be lighted from more than one angle to make it look three-dimensional.

Designers are acquainted with the psychological and emotional effects of lighting. For instance, they know that high-intensity light makes people generally more alert and that quick changes in lighting can be tiring.

There are three aspects of lighting. They are *color, intensity* and *distribution*. Warm colors more often are used for comedies, cooler colors in more serious plays. Colored light of one sort or another is almost always used because white light glares and hurts the eyes. Intensity refers to brightness and distribution to placement.

Lighting provides a constantly changing pattern and becomes a new design with each movement on the set, with each change in color, intensity or focus.

Once the designers figure out what is needed and what would help convey the mood or theme of the play, they make a lighting plot, which includes a mixture of general and specific lighting. They make an instrument schedule, which includes the instruments to use, where to hand them and where they should be focused.

Using a floor plan of the set they draw in the location of each instrument and the area the light will hit. Most of the time in a proscenium theatre the lights are placed overhead, at the rear of the auditorium and at various points along the sides of the auditorium.

The designer divides the stage into areas, using a minimum of two instruments for specific illumination in each area. This is to eliminate long shadows and light each side of the actor or set piece. Usually, the walls of a set are not well lighted since the reflected glare would hurt the audience's eyes. The designer also prepares a list of the lighting cues, so the technician knows exactly what to change and when.

Exercises

1. Use the scene you have worked with earlier and figure out what sorts of lighting instruments and what colors would help convey the mood of the play. Discuss this with the class.

2. Figure out if there is any way to use light to show location or time. Explain this to the rest of the class.

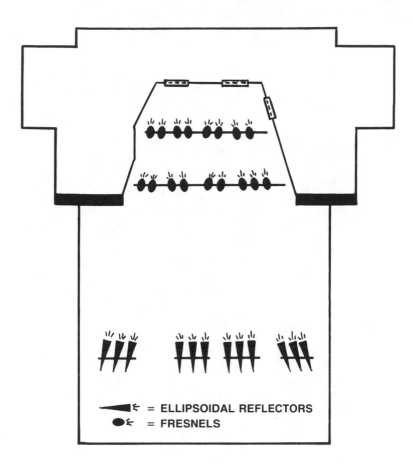

Here is a simplified lighting plot. Fresnels are above the stage; ellipsoidal reflectors are back in the auditorium.

CHAPTER NINE
Costumes and Make-up

Two of the designers who work on a production are concerned with how the actors look and how their appearance fits in with the scenery and lighting. They are the costume and make-up designers.

The Costume Designer

What people wear in everyday life tells us a lot about what they are like and often their occupations. The same carries over to characters in a play. Someone who wears bright colors and lots of jewelry is probably more of an extrovert than someone who dresses in softer colors and wears little jewelry. At the same time we can often tell a lot about a person's mood by what he or she wears. Some of this is subconscious. People who are happy generally dress in "happy" colors—pastels and bright clothing.

A person who wears jeans and T-shirts probably is more relaxed than someone who wears dressier clothes, though this, of course, often depends on the occasion. A man who wears casual clothes in the evening may dress in a business suit during the day because of his job.

Uniforms of all sorts tell us things about people. Not only can we tell what their jobs are, but we can assume things about their personalities because of these jobs. For example, when we see people in clerical collars we assume both that they are priests or pastors and also that they are devout. We also can assume that they care about others.

People in everyday life usually want to dress as others do, but there is a wide range in what this means, often depending on the circumstances. For instance, we almost certainly wouldn't wear shorts, open-necked white shirts and athletic shoes to church or to a school party. But they would be worn to play tennis.

Most people would feel uncomfortable wearing something that was totally different from what others were wearing for any particular event or occasion. Yet each of us wants to be an individual, which shows up in our clothing. Some women, for example, wear tiny earrings or none at all, while others wear big dangling earrings. Each of us expresses our personality through our clothing. Often people wear rings or T-shirts that have the name or logo of an organization to which they belong. This give them a sense of belonging but also of standing apart from others who do not belong.

Occasionally, you see people whose clothing is vastly different from everyone else's. For some reason, maybe as a kind of protest against something they think is wrong with society, they are total nonconformists in what they wear.

The costume designer has to keep all these things in mind about the characters in a play, who are individuals just like people in everyday life. The clothing the characters wear should help express their personalities, as well as telling us other things about them, such as occupation or circumstance.

Costuming, along with make-up, is the most individual and personal thing about a production's design. It provides the strongest hints about the personalities of the characters.

Like other areas of design, costumes should not usually call undue attention to themselves.

Planning the Costumes

Like all the other designers, the costume designers should know something about the other areas of theatre. They should be familiar with lighting design and color theory to understand which colors work together and which don't.

A costumer needs a flair for style and for what will look good on different people. What one person playing a particular character could wear might not be fitting for someone else in the same role.

The action of the play in part determines the costuming. It would be difficult for an actor wearing a heavy and cumbersome costume to act out a sword fight. Women unused to wearing floor-length dresses could have a lot of trouble going down steps. Straight skirts which make a character take short steps would probably be inappropriate for musicals where the characters have to dance.

Like the scene designer, the costumer often has to do historical research to find out the type of costumes worn in any period and then figure out how to *build* (in theatre, people "build" rather than "make" costumes) and maybe modify these costumes for the stage. They also need to know how light affects certain fabrics, making them richer or even duller looking.

Costuming has to fit the overall concept of the production. Bright costumes would go along with a bright-colored set, for example. Overall, the costume designer needs to be aware of color symbolism.

Often quick changes are required, so the designer should be able to build costumes that have tear-away seams and snaps and zippers instead of buttons, even though during the period in which the play is set, snaps and zippers hadn't yet been invented.

If the play is a period piece, the costumer begins by researching the historical period, its background, its people and its places to get a feeling for what things were like back then. The research is not just centered on the dress of the time but on attitudes and feelings of the population. In this way, the designer gains an idea of what each character should be wearing to reveal things not only about the personality but about the entire period as well.

The costumer meets with the other artists to work out an overall concept. This avoids clashes in color and style from one area of design to another. Then the costumer analyzes the script to understand the theme and the characters themselves.

Next come sketches such as this:

These are colored in to show the director and the other designers exactly what they will be like. The costumer also has to keep in mind which characters are the important ones overall and for each scene. In a musical, for example, the lead may have a much more elaborate costume than the chorus members, even though the costumes are similar. In other words, the costumer knows how to point up and emphasize characters through what they wear.

Last, the designer has to be well-acquainted with a wide range of fabrics. Some fabrics hang or drape differently from others. What sort of hang or drape is best for each character in each scene? Often the designer will attach a swatch of fabric to the sketches to show more clearly how the costume will look.

Exercises

1. Think of a friend. What can you tell about the kind of clothes he or she likes to wear?
2. Think of someone you don't especially like. What can you tell about this person by the type of clothes he or she wears?
3. Think of your social studies or math teacher. What sort of clothes does this person like? What does this say about his or her character?
4. Using the scene you have been working with or a new scene of your choice from somewhere in the book, either list or make a sketch of the type of clothing you think your characters should wear. Consider style, color and fabric. How do these costumes reveal the play's theme or subject matter? What do they reveal about each of the characters? Share what you have done with the rest of the class.
5. Decide who is the most important character for the scene. How would you point this out through costuming? Also discuss this with the class.

The Make-up Designer

Make-up and costumes both often help the actor feel the part. Make-up also can help identify the characters for an audience.

There are two types of make-up design: *straight* and *character*.

Straight Make-up

Straight make-up simply accentuates or enhances an actor's own appearance. Under theatrical lights a person's features tend to "wash out" or appear very pale. This is why a base make-up is used that is somewhat "warmer" or redder than the actor's own complexion.

The first thing applied for straight make-up is a *base* or foundation. This should be pretty consistent with—but a little warmer—than the actor's skin. Often theatrical make-up companies label the make-up not only by number but by type, for instance, "young man," "ruddy middle-aged man," and so on.

Although in past eras, grease paint was often used for the foundation, in most cases make-up now is water based. Called pancake make-up, it is similar actually to everyday make-up that women wear.

After the base is applied (usually by the actors themselves except if the make-up is complicated), features of the actor's face may be highlighted. Eyebrows and eyelashes most often are darkened, as are the rims of the eyes. Straight make-up is completed with a touch of rouge to the cheeks and lips.

Character Make-up

This type of make-up is used to change a character's appearance. An example would be a teenager playing the role of a grandmother or grandfather. Then, of course, the person has to look older. This can be done through a combination of things. One is by using hair spray—silver or white. Depending on the age of the person, all the hair can be touched up or maybe just the temples. The actor in the photo on page 139, for instance, looks much older than his actual age of 30.

Next, lines can be drawn or painted on the face to seem like wrinkles. The more wrinkles, the older the person. Certain features can be brought out or made more prominent through the use of highlighting. This means adding a touch of white to the base make-up. For example, the areas around the eyes can have a touch of white so they appear less sunken. With white, a nose can look a little larger than it really is.

Just the opposite of this is using black or brown make-up to made a facial feature recede or sink. This can make for sunken cheeks or hollow eyes, expressing the idea of fatigue, illness or starvation.

Crepe hair can be used to represent beards or moustaches. Crepe hair is made of wool or another fabric and usually comes in long strands which can be cut and shaped. Wigs and toupees also are used often to change appearance. Sometimes parts of the face are built up with the use of putty which could be applied to

A Gleason Photo, Kent, Ohio

This actor is made up to look 35 to 40 years older than he is.

the nose to make it long like Pinocchio's. Another method of changing the face is through the use of latex, a sort of rubber that can build up the cheeks or chin or other parts of the face. An example of character make-up used to completely alter appearance is shown on page 140.

Planning the Make-up

Make-up designers, like costumers, have to be acquainted with color theory and symbolism. They need to know how colored lights will alter the color of the make-up and what sorts of make-up complement the other areas of design. For stylized make-up the designers need to work closely with the other theatre artists so that all the designs mesh. Stylized make-up, for example, would look like the illustration on page 141.

For involved or difficult character make-up, designers prepare make-up charts. These are outlines of the face divided into areas and planes. The designers use them to indicate the color of

This actor's appearance is completely altered through the use of make-up.

make-up to be used and any special things to be done to each area. Sometimes a series is needed for a single actor who has to change appearances during the play, for example, aging gradually from a young person to an old one. An example of a make-up chart is shown on page 142.

Exercises

1. Using the scene you have been working with, decide which characters will need straight make-up and which, if any, character make-up. If you are to use character make-up, what changes will you need to make in the characters' appearance? When planning the make-up, assume that all your actors will be teenagers.
2. Prepare make-up charts for each of your characters, even if they do not require extreme changes in appearance. Indicate what kind of base make-up you would use. Next indicate the color of the make-up to be used

This photo shows the use of stylized make-up.

on the eyebrows and eyelashes. Generally, the lighter a person's hair coloring, the lighter the eye liner. The usual colors are light brown, dark brown and black.

3. If you have access to a makeup kit, make yourself up as one of the characters in your scene and make up another person as a different character.

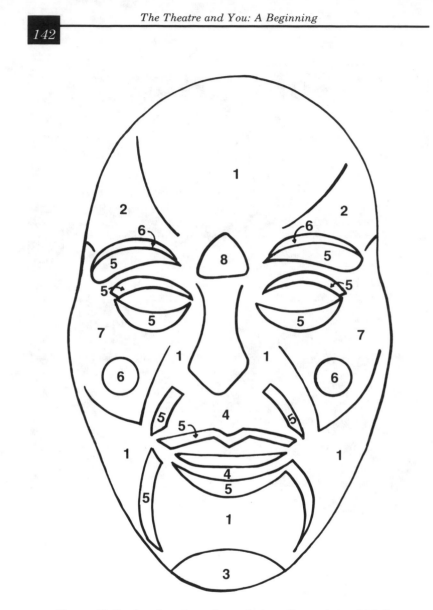

Along with the drawing, the make-up designer has a chart which lists the make-up to be used in each of the areas of the actor's face. Different areas are listed by number. For instance, the same color make-up would be used above and below the eyes and for other areas around the mouth.

The Audio Designer

Often called the sound engineer, this is the person who chooses any music to be used during the play, before it starts and at intermission. The audio designer also is responsible for any sound effects, like buzzing bees, car crashes, sirens, steamboat whistles and so on. Some of the sounds can be "live," but most are recorded. There are several companies that sell recordings of almost every imaginable sound.

The sound serves several purposes. Along with the visual aspects of the production, it can help create mood. Lively dance music, for example, can indicate an upcoming scene that is exciting or fast-paced. Certain classical music might prepare the audience for a serious show.

Exercises

1. Make a list of the sounds that either are needed for the production or would help set the mood of the scene with which you have been working.
2. With the same scene, choose music to be played at the beginning, at intermission and as the audience leaves the theatre.

The Property Master

The property master is the person who either designs or is responsible for finding or building the properties to be used in any production.

There are three types of props. The first is *set props*, which are the larger things that stand independently, such as furniture, trees and rocks. At times, these things are designed or chosen by the scene designer, and then the property master simply sees that they are available. At other times, the property master is the one who designs or chooses them.

The second type of properties is *set dressings*. These include paintings and other wall fixtures, vases and figurines. Usually the property master, rather than the scene designer, is responsible for choosing these.

The last type is *hand props*, anything the actors carry onstage or use while acting. These include such things as telephones, food, letters and silverware. It is up to the property master to choose hand props that are appropriate.

Exercises

1. Make a list of the set props that you would need for your scene. What style of furniture would be appropriate?
2. What types of set dressing would make the set for your scene look better? What makes you think so?
3. Make a list of all the hand props needed for your scene. Include anything you think might help establish mood or character, such as eyeglasses, a handkerchief and so on. Where would you be able to get them? Would they be easily available?

There are many other people besides the designers, director and actors who work on a production. Not even counting the *house staff* (those who handle the box office and do the ushering), nor the publicity people, there is a technical director, one or two stage managers and their assistants, crews to build costumes and sets, to hang the lights and do anything else necessary to prepare for opening night.

The technical director is responsible for all the visual and audio (except for the actors) aspects of the production. It is this person's job to see that the designers do their jobs and then to oversee all the other crews.

Often throughout the rehearsal of the show a stage manager sees that things run smoothly, that is, that the actors and crew members are present and ready to work when they should be. A stage manager then usually takes over everything beginning with the dress rehearsal, which signals the end of the director's preparations for opening night.

Many theatres hire a stage carpenter to oversee the building of sets.

Finally, there are running crews, including people who operate the lights. There are stagehands and members of the property crew who shift scenery and see that all properties are positioned where they should be backstage. However, it is the actors' final responsibility to see that they have all their props. This means that before each performance they need to check to see that everything is in place.

In order to do a good job in any area of theatre it helps to be acquainted with all the other areas so you can understand special problems and concerns.

Exercises

1. Of all the jobs described in this chapter, which interests you the most? Why?
2. Which job would you not like? Why?

PART IV
ACTING

CHAPTER TEN
Freeing Your Imagination

An actor is a person who has learned to imagine.

Learning to Use Your Imagination

In the imagination, an actor can be any other person it is possible to be.

Think what this means. Any time you want, you can be someone who lives in the sea, on another planet, or at the core of the earth. You can exist a million years in the future or five million years in the past. You can accomplish anything you want, have anyone as your friend. You can be an emperor, a space traveler, or a scientist who invents a pill to make everyone happy.

Every good actor can be in another person's body and mind, can become that person for two or three hours every evening, and then can bring everyone else into the world in which he or she now lives.

You have probably been told many times to stop daydreaming, to pay attention, to come back to the real world. In fact, many of us have been told this sort of thing so often that it is difficult to let the imagination go. Now is the time to disregard what you've been told. Now's the time to imagine, to create new worlds. This is what an actor does. It's the only way to be successful.

It would be impossible to get anywhere as an actor without using the imagination. It enters into every part of what an actor does, from "knowing" (imagining) how to feel in a certain situation to being able to see exactly how a character would deliver a line.

If you want to work on a play as any of the theatre artists you have to *remember* how to pretend. Young kids have no problem using the imagination, playing spaceman or house. They pretend/believe their stuffed animals are real, just like Hobbes is real to Calvin in the comic strip. But Hobbes comes to life only when he and Calvin are alone. Unfortunately, this is how life is for most of us, able only to pretend when we are by ourselves. This is because we've been told many times that the only way to get anywhere is through paying attention and being "practical." That is partly true, but there are also many times actors or designers or directors need to let the imagination soar.

Of course, there are times when we shouldn't let our daydreams get in the way—when we need to learn rules and hard facts. We need to memorize certain things by rote in order to multiply or divide or repeat lines in a play. We have to know about a particular historical period before we can imagine what it is like to be there. But in the imagining we need to use the part of our minds that is not so logical, that lets us do whatever we wish.

Using Both Logic and Creativity

These exercises should help you see that as an actor you need to use both the logical and the imaginative parts of your brain. You need to observe and study things and then use them in your imagination.

Exercises

1. We often expect people who dress a certain way to possess a certain type of personality. After school go to a store or a shopping center. For a minute or two watch someone you don't know, but don't get too close to them. Jot down what you think they might be like. Now move closer and eavesdrop on what they say. Were there any surprises? Do this with two or three people. What about them was just as you expected it to be? What was different? Now figure out what made you think of them in the way that you did.

2. To be a good actor you should get in the habit of observing people to learn how they act in different situations. The next time you go to a store or shopping center watch someone else for a minute or two. Then write down everything about them that you can remember. Read what you have written to the rest of the class. Have them ask for any other details you didn't mention.

3. Think of one of the people you have watched. Now pretend to be that person for 15 minutes. How did that make you feel? Do you think you were actually able to see the world as he or she did?

4. Try to learn at least two new things about your best friend, not things the person tells you but things you observe. Maybe the person has a different way of walking. Maybe it is something about the way he or she talks that you had not noticed before. Do the same thing with one of your family members, someone of a different

generation.

5. Show the class, through the way you move and talk, these new things you learned.

6. There is a belief that you can make yourself feel a certain emotion by making your face and body look like people do feeling that emotion. For instance, if you scowl and tense the muscles in your neck like someone who is angry, you can begin to feel angry. Try this with several different emotions. Do you think this works? Why or why not?

Recognizing First Responses

You probably also have been advised to take time before you leap into something. Think it through first; be cautious. This may be good advice for English and science homework and for taking exams, but bad advice when you are using your imagination. Many of our first responses are the most intuitive and honest. They most accurately indicate how we really feel. So if we try to squelch them, many good ideas are going to be lost.

You need to learn to recognize these first responses and then develop them. Many of them will not be good, but that does not matter. If you don't like them, you can come up with something else, some other way of creating a character or writing a play.

To learn to do this, try word association with yourself. (This, of course, is the same kind of thing you can do to create a character, either as an actor or a playwright. But here do not worry about that; simply let whatever happens come out.) Often we block what we are thinking because it may be silly or bad. Do this by yourself so nobody else can possibly think what you say is not a good thing.

Exercises

1. Begin with the word "black." What is the first word that comes to mind? The word after that? Do this with several other words, writing your responses on a sheet of paper. Use these words or others that each of your classmates comes up with:

    ball
    gun
    grandfather
    school

television

tree

2. Here is something else that can be fun to do, as well as helping you use your imagination. Write one word on three slips of paper. The words should be either nouns or adjectives, for example, car and grizzly. Now have your teacher collect the slips of paper and mix them up. You then should draw three from the pile, being sure not to get your own. Take the three words and in some way make up a story. For example, say the words are car, grizzly and moon. Then:

> My brother and I are in a *car*, and it runs out of gas in the mountains. There are no other cars around; the road is deserted. Just as we're about to get out and try to hitchhike or walk to the nearest gas station, a *grizzly* bear rushes toward us. We hurry back to the car. It is late afternoon. It's summertime, so we are hot and hungry. We wish the bear would go away. But it doesn't, not until the *moon* comes up. Then it lumbers down over the hillside. Even with the bear gone, my brother and I are afraid to leave the car, but finally another driver comes along and stops. We tell him we're out of gas, and he offers to take us to a service station and bring us back. Just as we're getting into the other person's car, the bear returns. "Where are you going?" the bear says, tears in his eyes. "I just wanted to play a game of Monopoly with you."

Use your imagination to make the story as silly or weird as you can.

3. This is a form of improvisation which you will learn more about later. Your teacher will bring a paper bag full of ordinary objects to class, things from around the house or school. Pick one of the objects out of the bag and pretend it is something else, something the real object reminds you of. For example, a chalkboard eraser can be a candy bar, a hairbrush, a bar of soap, a toy truck, a *Star Trek* communicating device or anything else your imagination lets it be. Now pass the object to a classmate and have that person pretend it is something else.

4. Pretend you are an animal. Be something more unusual

than a dog or cat or horse or cow. Do a silent imitation of the animal and have the class guess what you are.

In a play actors take what is there, and—out of their imaginations—add to it, making it unique. This is what makes theatre so magical. It is like the horse of a different color in *The Wizard of Oz*; things are always different, depending on who's playing the role.

Creativity and Playfulness

Many people who have studied the idea of creativity talk about the "playfulness" it involves. This is due to the sense of freedom that creating brings. But you lose some of the playfulness, the fun, if you feel inhibited or self-conscious about what you do.

The following are to help you learn to have fun with your imagination.

Exercises

1. Pretend you are the best-known actor in the world. A writer is interviewing you for the world's largest newspaper. Have a classmate play the part of the interviewer. What sort of things will you say during a two-minute interview?

2. Stand up and have someone else move you into a certain posture, including a way of holding your legs and arms and body. Keep this pose until you figure out the sort of person it makes you feel like. Tell the rest of the class what you feel and why you think you feel this way. Write a paragraph about the person you "became."

3. Again have someone place you in a particular pose. Now figure out a logical reason for the pose and follow through with a movement that will communicate exactly what you're doing. This should be something common like brushing your teeth or taking the clothes out of the dryer. Make sure the pose is an important part of the pantomime.

4. Now have a classmate place you in two separate poses. Logically go from one to the other, communicating an everyday or commonplace type of activity in the same way you did in exercise three.

5. Try to mirror the way two or three people walk and carry themselves, as well as mirroring their faces. How do you feel different now as a result of the imitations? Can you identify any better with these people now? If not, try the same thing again and again until you do feel different. If these are people you know, is there anything about what you did that makes you understand them better? Why or why not?

Using Emotional Memory

In the *System* of acting (developed by a Russian named Konstantin Stanislavski), which is a way of acting and getting into a character, there is a technique called emotional memory. The idea is that people really cannot remember emotions. Instead, we have to remember the circumstances, where we were, who else was there, and everything else we can about what happened. Only then do we begin to feel the emotion.

You can use emotional memory for a scene in a play, taking the emotion you felt in one set of circumstances and applying it to another set of circumstances.

Most often you really don't need to do this. It's a technique to use in case you are having trouble with a particular scene. But the idea can be helpful in trying to free your imagination.

Exercises

1. Try to remember a time you felt one of the following emotions. Try to remember the situation exactly:
    disgust
    sadness
    happiness
    grief
    frustration
    nervousness
    resentment
    Do you feel the emotion? If not, try again. Then take the feeling and write a short monolog (one-character) scene in which someone is feeling the same way. Now in front of the class, play the character you have created.
2. As a class, come up with different emotions. Have your teacher write them on the chalkboard. Choose an emo-

tion and ask someone else in the class to remember when they felt this way. Now come up with a situation in which a character could feel this emotion and have the person you chose portray for the class what happens as a result of being in this situation.

Acting is a combination of technique and "being" or feeling. It's been said that the best time for an actor to feel strong emotion is in the early stages of rehearsal. After that, you, as an actor, have to be in complete control or you risk not being convincing.

Being Sensitive to Self and Others

Anyone can be creative, so you must believe that you can be too. And the more strongly you believe, the more likely it is that you will be.

You can more easily create if you are aware of the world around you. To be an actor you have to be able to get outside yourself and see things from a lot of different viewpoints. At the same time you need to be aware of your own thoughts and feelings and attitudes. This is something people often don't try to do. But if you first are able to look deeply enough inside yourself to see how you feel, then you will have an easier time looking inside characters in a play.

An earlier exercise asked that you see something different about people you know well. This is because we normally don't do that sort of thing. We take people for granted and don't really look or listen.

Only if we are sensitive first to ourselves and to others can we begin to imagine how characters in a play feel. If we do look closely at others, then we are able to interpret and portray many different roles. The following are to help you become more aware and sensitive to what goes on around you.

Exercises

1. Work in pairs. Tie a blindfold around your eyes. For the next five minutes have a classmate guide you around the room and, if possible, into the hallway and outside. Your classmate should have you touch as many different objects as possible. Try to figure out, using only the sense of touch, what each one is. Now switch

and lead your partner around for five minutes.

2. Again close your eyes. Your teacher will time you. Listen very carefully for the next two minutes. How many different sounds can you hear? At the end of the two minutes write down how many things you heard. Your teacher will have everyone list all the different sounds. Are you surprised at how many there were? Were there sounds others heard that you didn't?

3. The reason for closing your eyes in each exercise is to block out one important sense to concentrate on other senses. This time when you close your eyes, think of how many things you can feel physically. To give you a few hints: How does your shirt or top feel against your neck? The seat against the back of your legs? Are you aware of any little itches or pains?

Besides emotional memory, there is something called *sense memory*. While emotional memory involves the way you feel inside, sense memory is how you feel outside. It has to do with things like hearing, smell, taste, touch and sight.

The reason for using sense memory is that it is another way to help you concentrate and become more aware of the world.

Sense memory also involves looking more closely at the ordinary. The next time you want to eat an orange, feel the weight of it in your hand, feel its texture, both the outer skin and the inside sections. Take a few moments to smell the orange, both the rind and inside. See all the differences of color. Then taste it and take time to think about the taste and how the orange feels on your tongue and in your throat. Is it warm or cool?

Learn to do this with all sorts of things—taking a shower, brushing your teeth, walking outside after a rain. Here are a few more specific things to try:

Exercises

1. Peel and eat a peach, an avocado or a banana. Experience each sensory detail as you do so. Just after you finish go over each step in your mind. Do the same with:
    chewing a piece of gum
    tasting lemon juice or vinegar
    climbing into bed and pulling up the covers
    eating a crispy apple

putting on a T-shirt or pullover sweater

drinking hot chocolate or ice-cold lemonade.

2. Now re-create one of these things without using the objects. Eat an apple in your imagination and show it through pantomime. Try to get it precisely right. Keep trying until you do.
3. Walk into a room at school or at home and take a minute to memorize everything you see. Now close your eyes and try to visualize what's there. Make as complete a list as you can. Then check to see how well you did. Do the same thing with a picture your teacher shows you.

Not everyone is naturally attuned to life. But you can develop sensitivity by doing exercises like the ones in the chapter. As a class or even by yourself, you can easily think up others.

Here are a few other things to help you develop your sensitivity to people.

Exercises

1. Imagine the next stranger you see as having a stuffy nose. Then do a pantomime of the person doing exactly what he or she was doing when you watched. But include the stuffy nose in the pantomime. The rest of the class should tell you how realistic you seemed to be.
2. Watch someone doing a job—washing dishes, sweeping, carrying a big container of bottled water or anything else. Memorize each step of the job. When you come to class, pantomime exactly what you saw and have the class try to figure out what you're doing.
3. Go to a shopping mall or a large department store or supermarket. Try to discover five distinctive things about every third person you see there, things about the person's appearance or about what he or she was doing. Keep a record of these traits. Then report to your class what the person was like and what the traits were.

Learning to Be Flexible

There are many, many ways to play a character, which means you never have to be bound by one idea. Instead you should be willing to experiment. With many things in life, it's often difficult to realize that one method of doing something works just as well as another method. For example, some countries measure things in feet and miles, others in meters and kilometers. Yet, each person knows how far it is from point A to point B.

If you find that one way of playing a character is not working as well as you like, try another way. You can do this by "twisting your thinking." Add a different character or physical trait such as the stuffy nose. Then take the trait away. The character still should be changed at least a little from the first way you played him or her.

You have time to do this after being cast in a play. As you learned in an earlier chapter, a lot of the rehearsal schedule is planned for developing and building a character.

Stimulating Creativity in Acting

There are many ways of stimulating the imagination in learning to act.

One is to establish an entire characterization on the basis of a single trait. If you are improvising a character, you may decide that he moves his hands slowly and precisely. Then you ask why. You decide his arms are somewhat stiff and cause him pain. Why? He is now in his 20s. Years ago, as a teenager, he was painting his parents' house and fell off the ladder, breaking both arms. Because they were set wrong, they never healed properly. Continue with the questions. How did this affect him? Is he angry and bitter? Why? Because the accident occurred just before he was to go to college on a baseball scholarship. Not only was he hoping to play ball professionally, but it was the only way he could afford to go to college. For the next few years he did nothing, moping around the house, refusing to get a job, taking his bitterness out on his father who had insisted he paint the house.

You can go on and on until you come up with a complete character which you now understand just by choosing a random trait and asking questions about it.

You can use this sort of thing for writing, acting, designing and so on. It is called playing the "what if " game. What if I knew someone who used his hands precisely? And what if it was the result of an accident?

In the following just let your imagination go.

Exercises

1. Take this situation and carry it on out until a character or setting or scene begins to take shape. What if you saw a big farmhouse surrounded by evergreen trees? And what if it looked peaceful and secure? But what if . . . You decide what happens from here on.
2. What if you went home from school one day and something about your house or apartment looked funny? What if you peeked through the door? And what if the furniture there was not your family's . . . Take this on as far as you can.
3. What if one of your teacher's is really an alien from a different galaxy? And what if this person took the job at school . . .
4. Think up the beginning of a "what if " situation. Now exchange papers with someone else and let your imagination go.

If you are interpreting a character from a play, you still can try to discover a trait that can provide a key or even the entire basis to your interpretation of the role. In the following scene from a play called *The Last Vampire*, for instance, you might play Gordonov as a "toucher," the sort of person who always touches someone's hand or shoulder or arm while talking. This is logical because Gordonov, as one of the lines implies, has not let himself be close to anyone because he has outlived all the friends he ever made. Now he is feeling bad about it.

1
2
The Last Vampire
3 **CHARACTERS:** JEANNIE, late twenties; GORDONOV,
4   looks thirty but is centuries older.
5 **SETTING:** The action occurs in Jeannie's apartment which
6   she shares with her father. She and Gordonov are alone.
7 **AT RISE:** As the scene opens, JEANNIE and GORDONOV
8   are sitting at the table drinking coffee.
9
10 GORDONOV: **I love you. It's as simple as that.**
11 JEANNIE: *(Shrugs)* **We've been seeing each other for—**

1   what?—six months. I know absolutely nothing about
2   you.
3   GORDONOV: What would you like to know?
4   JEANNIE: Well, for starters, where are you from?
5   GORDONOV: I was born in Europe. I'm not sure exactly
6   where. *(JEANNIE looks at him strangely and frowns.)*
7   My mother said I was born in the Ukraine. But I don't
8   remember living there. I remember the lights of Paris,
9   the Cathedral of Notre Dame. And the Black Forest.
10   I remember that. And South Africa and Spain and
11   Scandinavia.
12   JEANNIE: I don't understand.
13   GORDONOV: You won't believe what I tell you.
14   JEANNIE: Try me.
15   GORDONOV: *(Pause)* All right. I'm a vampire.
16   JEANNIE: What?!
17   GORDONOV: I didn't expect you to believe me.
18   JEANNIE: You're serious, aren't you? You're not
19   kidding.
20   GORDONOV: You probably think I'm crazy. But I've
21   lived in a hundred places, had a score of careers. In
22   most ways I'm just like you.
23   JEANNIE: *(Pulling a sweater from the back of the chair and*
24   *slipping it around her shoulders)* **If this is a joke, you've**
25   **carried it much too far.**
26   GORDONOV: Would it help to say I'd do anything to be
27   like you. *(Pause)* I never thought I'd say that. I vowed
28   I'd never become involved with anyone ever again.
29   I've had too many disappointments. Too many
30   friends have died.
31   JEANNIE: I don't know why you're doing this. I suppose
32   you must believe it. And God knows, I still love you.
33   GORDONOV: I have an idea. *(Glancing at his watch)* I'll
34   show you where I live.
35   JEANNIE: Where you live?
36   GORDONOV: Yes. A three-room house. A cottage. With

1   a waterbed. I don't sleep in a coffin. And I don't sleep
2   all day. I do a lot of work at night. Only because it's
3   cooler then and quiet. I write historical novels. Why
4   not? I've lived in the times I write about. *(Pause)* I
5   sleep till ten or ten-thirty and then get up. The
6   daylight doesn't harm me.
7 JEANNIE: You still insist all this is true?
8 GORDONOV: Oh, yes. It's true.

In observing other people, we can see how each reacts differently to various situations. We can then take a trait from each of them and use it in creating a character. It is just like when we empathize with a friend who has a problem. We can put ourselves in the place of the friend and feel some of what the friend is feeling.

What all this means is that we can look at characters in new ways which can help us discover something previously hidden from us. This is just a starting point. We may then drop the extraneous trait. On the other hand, if we find the trait is a valid part of the characterization and seems to work, we can keep it.

CHAPTER ELEVEN
Improvisation

Improvisation means playing a character or a scene without a script.

There are two types: Creating new scenes with a character from a play, and creating a new character and scene.

Improvising with Existing Characters

Sometimes you play a character that comes from a play, but you create scenes that are not part of the script. Suppose you were playing the title role in *The Diary of Anne Frank*, a play about a teenager hiding from the Nazis during World War II, for the audience you would "be" only the Anne Frank who is confined to the upper story of a house day after day.

Of course, there is more to Anne than the part that appears in the scenes from the play. She didn't suddenly come to life as a complete person. So in order for you, as an actor, to understand her more completely, the director might ask you to create a scene where it is a month or so earlier and Anne is going shopping with her mother and meets one or two of her friends.

Some directors like to start each rehearsal by having the actors improvise scenes among themselves. Everyone plays the same character but in scenes "outside" the script. The idea is to "see" how the character behaves in other situations so the actor can better understand the type of person he or she is playing.

A different way of looking at this kind of improvisation is that it helps you play the character more "fully," because you have a better understanding of the person. But you do have to be consistent, that is, you have to try your best to do the improvisational scenes as your character would do them, rather than as you yourself would.

Sometimes a director will call rehearsals during the run of a show, particularly if it's a long run, and have the actors do this type of improvisation. The reason for this is that there is a risk of a performance becoming "stale," or lacking "sparkle." It is easy for an actor to get into a rut because the show and the role have become familiar.

Improvising with their characters outside of the play can help actors to bring back the "freshness," which is important in keeping an audience interested. Even though the actor has performed the role many times, it is always the *first* time for the character who is "living" the action and the first time for members of the audience.

Another reason for creating a scene with your character is to understand how it feels to "experience" something that is referred to but not actually included in the script. In the exercises that follow there's a scene from *The Closing of the Mine* where Billy mentions that Bob, one of his friends, has to move to New York because his father cannot find a job. The scene where Bob and Billy talk about this is not included in the play, but a director might have the two characters improvise the scene so they can "experience" the feelings of loss and sadness this brings.

Exercises

1. Here are scenes from two plays. Using what is already there as the basis for improvisation, play one of the characters with someone else and build a new scene.

1   Scene One — **Going Steady**
2
3   *CHARACTERS:* MARTIN, KAREN, MR. HIGGEN-
4   BOTHAM.
5   *SETTING:* The action occurs in a junior high classroom
6   where the students have been given time to complete
7   a history assignment while MR. HIGGENBOTHAM
8   grades papers. It is the last period of the day.
9   MARTIN sits two rows over from KAREN.
10   *(As the curtain rises, MARTIN is looking at an*
11   *antique watch that belonged to his great-great-*
12   *grandmother. He brought it to school as part of a*
13   *history assignment. KAREN is totally absorbed in*
14   *watching MARTIN. In a moment KAREN passes*
15   *MARTIN a note asking to see the watch. MARTIN*
16   *shakes his head no.)*
17
18   **KAREN:** *(Mouthing the words)* **Please. I just want to**
19   **look at it.**
20   **MARTIN:** *(Whispering)* **I'm sorry, Karen. I don't**

1 **want anything to happen to it.**
2 **KAREN:** *(Turning down the corners of her lips)* **Please,**
3 **Martin, please.**
4 **MARTIN:** *(He sighs, picks up the watch and hands it*
5 *across to her.)* **Be careful. Mom would kill me if**
6 **anything happened to it.**
7 **KAREN:** *(Holding the watch)* **Thank you. You're a**
8 **very nice boy.**
9 **MARTIN:** *(He hits the heel of his palm against his*
10 *forehead.)* **Oh, man.** *(MR. HIGGENBOTHAM looks*
11 *up and then goes back to grading the papers.)*
12 **KAREN:** *(She opens the back of the watch and reads the*
13 *inscription.)* **For Jonathan from his loving wife,**
14 **Thelma Eisenstadt. Philadelphia, Pennsylvania.**
15 **December 25, 1863.** *(She looks at MARTIN.)* **How**
16 **sweet.**
17 **MARTIN:** **Give it back, Karen.**
18 **KAREN:** **In a minute. Just as soon as—***(The dismissal*
19 *bell rings.)*
20 **MR. HIGGENBOTHAM:** **All right class. We'll start**
21 **with the row by the window. You're dismissed.**
22 **MARTIN:** **Darn!** *(He whispers as loudly as he can.)*
23 **Karen.**
24 **MR. HIGGENBOTHAM:** **That's enough, Martin.**
25 *(MARTIN grits his teeth and glances at KAREN who*
26 *places the watch in her purse.)*
27 **MARTIN:** **Karen, for heaven's sake, give it to me.**
28 **MR. HIGGENBOTHAM:** **Next row. You're**
29 **dismissed.**
30 **KAREN:** *(Rises and smiles sweetly at MARTIN.)* **'Bye,**
31 **'bye.**
32 **MARTIN:** *(Speaking through clenched teeth)* **Give it to**
33 **me.** *(He wants to go after KAREN but knows he can't.*
34 *He watches KAREN leave the room, then sinks back*
35 *into his seat.)*

1   Scene Two — **The Closing of the Mine**

2

3   *CHARACTERS:*   BILLY, 16; DAN, his father; HELEN,

4   his mother.

5   *SETTING:* The action occurs in the kitchen of the

6   O'Jenkins' house in a small coal-mining area of

7   Western Pennsylvania. It is the early 1950s. At

8   Center is a battered wooden table covered with

9   oilcloth. Around it are three wooden chairs. Up Left

10   is a coal-burning kitchen stove and Up Right is a

11   chipped porcelain sink. A door Stage Right leads to

12   the outside, another door Up Left leads to the upstairs.

13   Down Left is a little stand with a phone.

14   *(As the curtain rises, BILLY, DAN and HELEN are*

15   *eating dinner.)*

16

17   **BILLY:**   Bob told me he's going to move to New York

18   and won't get to finish school here.

19   **DAN:**   There'll be no work here when the mine shuts

20   down. The men have to go where they can find

21   jobs.

22   **HELEN:**   Lizzie told me the company's going to sell

23   the houses. She heard they're asking $400, just

24   to get rid of them.

25   **DAN:**   If that's true, I don't know where we'll get

26   the money. *(He takes a sip of his coffee.)* It may just

27   be a rumor, but I doubt it. If the company were

28   doing OK, they wouldn't have let us stay here.

29   **BILLY:**   What do you mean, Dad?

30   **DAN:**   The town was built by the company for their

31   employees. Yet they let us live here even after I

32   quit and started to teach music. They saw the

33   future; they knew the shutdown was coming.

34   **HELEN:**   They should have let us know.

35   **DAN:**   And have the miners quit on them before they

36   were ready to close? You know they'd never do

1		that. *(He takes a bite of fried potato.)* **They're in**
2		**business to make money, not to act as social**
3		**workers.**
4	**HELEN:**	**It seems like a rotten thing to do.**
5	**BILLY:**	**I asked Bob if he couldn't stay with someone.**
6	**HELEN:**	**Who would he stay with? Just about**
7		**everyone is going to be leaving.**
8	**DAN:**	**There's already a sense of panic. Men angry,**
9		**frustrated. Talking but not able to take any**
10		**action. They've always looked to the Union. But**
11		**the days of John L. Lewis are over and done with.**
12	**HELEN:**	**I guess we're pretty lucky that you have**
13		**other work.**
14	**DAN:**	**Yeah, the other men here—they've been**
15		**miners all their lives, most of them. It's**
16		**especially tough for the older men. Even the**
17		**young ones—the few that are still here—are in**
18		**for a rough time. The young fellows who left,**
19		**they're the smart ones.** *(The phone rings and*
20		*BILLY gets up to answer.)*
21	**BILLY:**	**Hi, Ruthie. . . . What's wrong? Why are you**
22		**crying? . . . What?! . . . Why are you—** *(He listens*
23		*for a few more moments.)* **Oh, God.** *(He comes back*
24		*to the table.)* **Can I be excused?**
25	**HELEN:**	**What's wrong, Billy?**
26	**BILLY:**	**It's Ruthie; she has to move to Pittsburgh.**
27		**I hate the mine. I hate the coal company.** *(He*
28		*turns and races to the Stage Right door. He exits.)*

Sometimes directors will have the actors in a play switch roles either using the script or in improvisation. This is so each person can better understand the thoughts and feelings of other characters and why they act as they do.

Creating New Characters

The second type of improvisation involves creating something completely new with only certain "given circumstances."

This means that the actors are told that certain things are so. Then they have to take these things, make them part of the scene and go on from there. For example, a director tells you and another person that it is late at night, you two are teenagers alone in a big house out in the country and you hear someone trying to break in. You know that a very dangerous criminal has escaped from a nearby hospital for the criminally insane. Besides all that, a storm has interrupted phone and electrical service. Taking all that and anything else the director tells you into consideration: How do you react? What do you do?

Given circumstances include any background information you need to understand the situation, the scene, the action or the characters. It can include: 1) the setting, such as a big house in the country; 2) the area, such as the slum area of a large city or the Arctic Circle; 3) the historical period, such as the Middle Ages or the 22nd century; 4) the finances of the characters, for example, if they're extremely wealthy or so poor they're homeless; 5) the conditions of the country or the world, such as being in the middle of a great plague, or when a mad dictator has taken control of North America. You need to take each of these things into consideration when creating a scene because each could affect the action.

Given circumstances can include information about each character. For example, make one of the characters in the big house in the country a person confined to a wheelchair. Or make the person have a severe hearing or speech handicap. How might this affect the action?

Fulfilling Intentions

Many times the director will tell you your "intentions" in an improvisational scene. This means your character's goal in being there and the reason for wanting to reach the goal. Each important character has a purpose or an action to perform or a purpose to achieve in each scene. Your intention is the reason behind what you do.

For instance, in the house where someone is breaking in, your intention may be to escape. But how would you present a scene based on the same set of circumstances if the criminal were your father. You love him and haven't seen him in years and yet you don't want your friend to find out that he is your father. Your intention is to help him escape while not letting your friend know this. Or suppose it isn't the criminal outside but another friend, and you've decided to play a joke on the other person in the house by frightening him or her. Your intention then, of course, is to scare your friend. But why? Maybe this is part of the given circumstances, maybe it isn't. Maybe you think it would be great fun to frighten someone this way. Or maybe you're mad at the person and want to get even for something.

Going Steady is about a girl who takes an antique watch from a boy and then tells her friends: "Martin gave me his watch because we're going steady." This obviously isn't true. The reason or intention for the lie is never stated, so it is up to the actress playing the role to figure out what it is.

It may be that Karen feels unloved and this is a way of pretending someone cares about her. Or maybe she's angry at Martin and does this to "put him on the spot." Or maybe she likes Martin so much that in her fantasies they really are going steady. Then by taking the watch and lying to her friends, she is trying to talk herself into believing that what she says really is true.

The rest of the play shows that Karen and Martin probably do like each other, although Martin is very angry—more so that she took the watch than that she lied. The intention depends on how you think of your character. That is one reason no actor plays a role exactly as anyone else would.

Intentions in improvisation sometimes are easy to understand because the director tells you what they are. Yet often, you are not told the other persons' intentions. Again, taking the situation of the person trying to break in, maybe your intention is to help him escape from the police (the goal) because you think he isn't guilty (the reason or intention). The other character may want to become a hero by capturing him dead or alive (the goal) so everyone will now respect him or her (the intention).

The idea of scenes like this may be to: 1) help you build a particular character, 2) to learn to concentrate, or 3) to gain confidence in seeing that you are able to get through a scene and make it believable.

Improvisational scenes make you fit yourself into others' shoes and to think and react as *they* would, rather than as you would.

The scenes also help you to see that you are free to use whatever memories and feelings you have to make the situation and actions believable. In other words, it helps you to free your imagination.

Intention shows through action the thoughts and feelings of a character. Later you will learn to analyze a character in a play. Figuring out the intention is a large part of this.

Many times you cannot find the intention just by reading

the lines. You have to know the characters to understand how they think and reason.

The intention may match the action, but it doesn't have to. Suppose a female character wants to get a male character to do something. In her dialog the woman flatters the man, telling him how wonderful he is, how handsome, how intelligent. But underneath all this she feels contempt or disgust. This is exactly what happens in the comedy, *The Miser*, by Molière where a matchmaker named Froisine tries to get Harpagon, the miser, to marry Marianne.

Exercises

1. Figure out the intentions and the actions and perform the following scene:
   Setting—a city park, early afternoon, summer.
   Characters—a man and a woman in their 20s, dressed in jeans or shorts and T-shirts.
   Action—the woman stands on the sidewalk; the man lies on the grass. The woman demands that the man get up. He refuses.
   There can be many different intentions here. For instance: 1) the man has been injured, and the woman is frantic with worry. She wants him to get up so she'll know he's OK. 2) They are married, and he wants to take time to enjoy the beautiful weather, while she wants to go shopping. 3) They have just had a fight and neither will give in.
   Take the same scene and give the character's different backgrounds and motivations. Change the intentions and the backgrounds once more and do still another scene.

2. Figure out a new situation, characters and action. Choose two classmates to determine intentions and play the scene.

3. Work with original scenes you have written or with scenes your teacher brings to class. The teacher will tell each of you your reasons for behaving as you do but will not tell any other characters who will appear in the scene with you. Now perform the scene, really listening and paying attention to the other actors. Decide how your character would change his or her behavior as a result of what you find out as the scene progresses.

Learning to Listen

When you do improvisational scenes, you learn to be sensitive to the other "characters" and learn to listen closely to what they say.

Part of the reason actors often "go stale" is that they stop listening. In improvisation, just as in life, you have to listen to what people are saying to you so you will be able to respond to them in a believable or proper way.

Sometimes actors in improvisational scenes become so concerned over what they will say and do that they stop listening and reacting to the others in the scene. Yet most often in life, unless you're particularly worried or nervous, you aren't concerned about what you'll say.

In plays, in life and in improvisational scenes, your responses usually bear directly on what someone has just said to you.

If you learn to listen and respond in improvisation, then you should be able to do it easily in a scripted scene. The improvisational scenes can help you see that you can be in control and there is no need to be afraid of what will happen on-stage. You also learn to see that your character has a life separate from yours, and as that character you can have contact and communicate with others in a realistic or truthful manner.

It is very important to give an improvisational scene direction rather than just letting it ramble on. This is where you have to keep your intentions in mind. Then when one of the characters "wins" by reaching his or her goal, you need to end the scene as quickly as possible.

Once you know the given circumstances you should take a few moments to think about them and to decide what is important about your character and the scene that was not "given."

When you improvise, there is no need to worry about whether the scene is original. Just do what comes to mind. If you are really listening and paying attention to the other people in the scene, most of the time what you do will be original.

Exercises

1. Your teacher will provide you with given circumstances and intentions for a two-character improvisational scene that is to last two minutes. You should not know the other person's intention. But listen carefully so at

the end of a minute you can switch roles and continue as the other character to the end.

2. Your teacher will give you another two-character scene in which you and the other person have goals that are exactly opposite of each other. An example might be: You want very much to see a certain movie that is playing only for one day, while your friend wants very much to go to an important basketball game at your school. Play the same scene two different ways. One of the two times you refuse to give in, no matter what. Since this is the case, how can you logically end the scene? The second time you let your friend talk you into doing what he or she wants. Even though you want to do the other thing, something makes you give in. What is it?

3. Take *Going Steady* or *The Closing of the Mine* and begin with what is already written. Then extend the same scenes for two more minutes.

4. Play an improvisational scene in which you and another person are opposed. With the other person in your scene, figure out what "given circumstances" you think are important. Play the scene as:

   a. a hard-of-hearing grandmother and a teenager who always wants his or her way.

   b. a teacher who has given a low grade he or she is convinced is deserved and a student who thinks he or she deserves a higher grade.

   c. a bank robber holed up with a hostage and the hostage whose young child is severely ill.

   d. two characters and a situation you and a classmate plan yourselves.

CHAPTER TWELVE
Using Your Body

There are many ways of establishing a proper frame of mind for creating. One is to imagine yourself in a place where you can be completely at ease. Maybe it's the bank of a stream under the cool shade of leafy trees, or in the yard of a big old farmhouse, away from anyone who can boss you around.

The more you create in your mind, the easier it becomes to relax and enter into the creative state. You can imagine yourself wherever you like, in whatever place is the most soothing.

You can do physical exercises to help you relax. Directors sometimes have a different actor lead the cast in a few minutes of exercising before each rehearsal or performance. Or you can take a few minutes to do it yourself. Here are a few you might try.

Exercises

1. Stand and stretch one leg in back and the other in front, bent at the knee. Lean forward and then back. Now switch the leg in front with the one in back and rock gently back and forth.

2. Gently roll your head over one shoulder, around back and then to the front, letting it hang limp. Then reverse the direction. Do this twice in each direction. Then stop or you may begin to feel dizzy.

3. Yawn. At the same time stretch your arms and arch your back to stretch the muscles there.

4. Hunch up your shoulders. Now move them forward, to the middle once more and then to the back.

5. Place your hands one to two inches apart on the back of your neck. Now massage your neck up and down and in circles.

6. Figure out which part of your body feels the most tension. Maybe it's your neck, your shoulders or your hips. Make that area as tense as possible, then quickly let go of all the tension.

As an actor, you not only affect yourself when you are tense, but you affect the other actors and the audience as well.

Instead of transmitting your tension to others, try transferring it to objects—a doorknob, a prop, a railing. That does not mean that you should grip the object hard. Instead, visualize the tension flowing from you into the object just like electricity flows from an electric cord into a lamp.

Here are some more ways you can begin to feel relaxed.

Exercises

1. Let your arms hang loose at your sides. Then imagine the tension flowing from your body into your arms and down to the fingers. Then shake the tension out.
2. Imagine you are traveling through your own bloodstream. Take along a magic purifying agent that restores energy at the same time it rids the body of tension.

The best thing about these exercises is that they stretch the imagination at the same time they relieve tension and help you concentrate. Now try to think up two or three of your own exercises. Your teacher may ask you to lead the rest of the class in doing them.

How Creative Concentration Helps

Have you ever noticed that when you are having fun or enjoying a movie or television show that you rarely think of yourself? This means you are completely engrossed in what you are doing.

The same thing should happen when you are acting. If you don't worry about yourself and how you are doing, you're much more likely to be playing the part well.

The following exercises will help develop concentration.

Exercises

1. This is an old game. One person says, "I'm going on a vacation, and I'm taking with me . . ." The object has to be something that begins with the letter "A." The next person repeats what the first has said and adds something that begins with the letter "B." The game can be continued through the alphabet as many times

as the players are able to remember all the answers. As people forget, they have to drop out. The winner is the person who is left.

2. Read a newspaper story aloud while someone is telling you an entirely different story. At the end tell the class what you read and also tell the story you heard.

3. Rub your belly and pat your head. At the end of 10 seconds switch to patting your belly and rubbing your head. At the end of another 10 seconds switch once more. Have someone call the times for you.

4. Do a mirror exercise. Stand facing a classmate and try to duplicate his or her movements exactly as they would be seen in a mirror. Halfway through the exercise, switch. You lead and have the other person follow, but do not make the switch apparent.

5. Play the game of "Murder." Sit in a circle. Your teacher will have you choose slips of paper. On one is the letter "M" for murderer. On the others is "V" for victim. The object is for the murderer to "kill" the victims before they catch him or her. The victims, of course, want to stay alive. The murderer kills the victims by winking at them. As soon as the victims see the murderer wink at them, they have to lower their heads and not make eye contact with anyone else. The victims, while trying not to be killed, attempt to catch the murderer winking at someone else. If they do, they say, "I accuse [the person's name] of murder." The victim who solves the mystery wins. If no one catches the murderer, he or she wins. If you accuse someone who is not the murderer, the penalty is "death."

All the exercises for relaxation and concentration make us better able to communicate both with our bodies and voices.

Body Language

Our bodies are constantly communicating our thoughts and feelings. We actually communicate more nonverbally than with the use of words. We do this with facial expression, posture and carriage, gestures, touching and how much room we leave between ourselves and other people. Your body can reveal your personality, show how you are feeling and convey whether or not you are telling the truth verbally.

In the same way we learn words and verbal language through imitation, we learn as infants and children what certain nonverbal signs mean. Yet even when we know these signs, we often give ourselves away by communicating feelings that we would just as soon others did not pick up on.

We have been taught what certain gestures mean—such as nodding and shrugging. But there are many other things we need to be aware of as actors. They often provide more "meat" to a characterization than do actual words. What does it mean for instance to drag our feet?

What do the people in these photos convey about their feelings?

What feelings do you think these actors are conveying?

In the following try to show feelings without exaggeration and without the use of words.

Exercises

1. Convey a feeling of happiness.
2. Show a feeling of tiredness.
3. Tell the rest of the class that you are relaxed and feeling good.
4. Convey embarrassment.
5. Convince the class that you are extremely nervous.
6. Think of a different feeling or emotion and convey it to the rest of the class. Have them try to figure out what it is.
7. Think of another feeling and write it down on a slip of paper. Exchange your paper with someone else and convey the feeling your classmate indicated.

Communicating as Character and as Self

When we act, we have to be careful that we communicate as the character we're playing and not so much as ourselves. We have to stay in character and yet communicate as a performer.

As actors, we cannot let our personal lives interfere with what we do on stage. We cannot let the audience know that in our own lives we have problems and worries because, of course, the character would not have them.

It is our job as actors to determine our character's physical traits, liabilities, habits and feelings. These things have to be consistent with what the playwright has written. We need to be able to portray a variety of physical characteristics and make them believable. Our acting wouldn't be effective if we couldn't convince the audience we were deaf in *Children of a Lesser God*, blind and deaf like Helen Keller in *The Miracle Worker* or physically deformed like the lead character in *The Elephant Man*.

Of course, we cannot always be aware of everything we are communicating because we are ourselves and not the characters, yet these personal things should be subtle enough so that they don't detract from our acting.

Exercises

1. Choose a partner. One of you should assume a facial expression that shows a certain emotion. The other person should then try to show the same emotion in a different way. Now switch and do the same thing again.
2. Now do the same thing through posture and carriage.

Gestures

There are four types of gestures people use to communicate. There are those that: 1) direct or indicate; 2) describe or illustrate; 3) express or emphasize, and 4) reveal something about self.

The first type includes pointing, beckoning, shaking the head or waving someone away. Many directive gestures are exact and unvarying, except from one culture to another. For instance, waving your hand toward someone in the United States means "good-by." In some Eastern cultures it means "come here."

The second kind of gesture is less accurate. But when it is used with words it is usually clear. We hold out our hand, palm down, to say: "The child is this tall." What are some possible meanings for the gesture shown below?

The third type is for emphasis. We shrug or stamp our feet to point out what we say with words. What do you think the people below could be saying when using these gestures?

The last type of gesture is meant only for self, but often is the same one we use to communicate to someone else. We tap a foot, grimace or clench our fists in reaction to something else. Often we aren't even aware we're doing them. What can you tell about the people in the photo below?

All these sorts of gestures can add a lot to the interpretation of a character. Of course, they have to fit the character's personality and the circumstances.

For some strange reason, speakers, actors and singers often worry about what to do with their hands, which, of course, people rarely do in everyday life. Because of this they call attention to their hands or else appear awkward, usually when standing. To change this, just think of what you do in everyday life and adapt this to the character you are playing.

People who are nervous also tend to make tiny gestures that not only are hard to see but are down too low, like this:

This type of gesture calls attention to itself because it looks so silly or unnatural. It also tells more about the actor than about the character.

Carriage and Posture

We can see that a person who sits with feet under a chair, shoulders rounded and arms clasped in front of the chest, in all probability is not open to conversation. Unless we know more about the situation, we cannot deduce exactly what the body language is saying, except that it is negative. It could mean the person is depressed, ashamed or guilty.

On the other hand, if a person sat in the chair, legs stretched out in front and hands resting on the arms of the chair, we would think he or she was open to conversation.

Hundreds of positions and carriages are easy to understand in a broad sense and can add to the role in a play if they are done in character.

Movement

The third type of body language is movement, either while standing still or in going from one spot to another. We communicate nervousness by playing with a lock of hair or a button. We communicate happiness by a springy step.

Exercises

1. Communicate a mood or feeling to the rest of the class through the use of gestures.
2. Do the same thing through the way you stand or by moving from one spot to another.
3. Now take all three types of movement and present a 30-second scene in which you communicate at least three things about the character you are playing.

Many actors take specialized classes in such areas as fencing, dancing or martial arts to be able to play a big variety of roles. Whether you take the classes or not, you need to exercise regularly to be in shape for any physical requirements of a role. Best are aerobic exercises because they involve moving the whole body through space. They include such things as jogging, swimming and biking.

Filling Space

The way we come across as actors depends in part on how we fill space. Each of us is an element in a kind of sculpture, made up of everyone and everything on the stage.

The setting, the stage and the seating areas are altered each time we move. Around each of us is a globe of space.

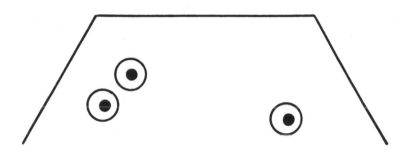

Each of us has a globe of space which usually separates us from others.

Our particular globe of space might be smaller or larger than another character's, depending on the type of person we are portraying. Think of this globe as a bubble that often remains separate from other bubbles. At times then there are as many bubbles on stage as there are actors. But this is not always the case.

If people are in a close relationship, like mother and child or husband and wife, the bubbles merge:

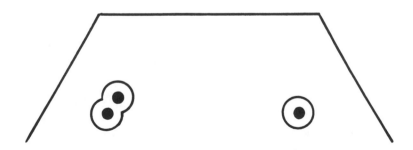

The merged globes of space mean the two characters
Stage Right are emotionally close.

The same thing happens in life. People usually stay a distance away from others unless they are close emotionally. Depending on the circumstances the bubble shrinks or expands. If we ride a bus, we often have to share a seat with someone else. But once off the bus, the bubble expands. We usually do not invade the space of other people, especially strangers; we mind our own business.

Each person is entitled to his or her own space in the classroom, on the street or anywhere else. The bubble or globe cannot shrink too far and remain that way, or there will be conflict. Neither can it expand too far, for most of us would not be able to stand the loneliness.

In many cultures, personal space is smaller than in the United States. Americans would feel uncomfortable standing as close in conversation as many from other cultures stand. Yet even in these countries, it is taboo to go beyond a certain point.

Most often we are responsible, both as individuals and actors, for our own space. Even in group scenes, with three or more actors occupying a certain portion of the stage, the bubbles or globes would look something like this:

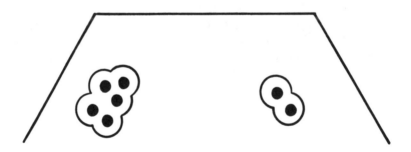

People who are not emotionally close keep their own globes
of space even when they are physically close.

Much of how we fill space on stage depends on the director's blocking of the show. Yet some of this is up to us as actors.

A good rule is: The more powerful the individual the larger the globe. Presidents and queens would have much bigger globes than servants.

Exercises

1. Take the character of Sir Harry in *The Twelve-Pound Look* and figure out how big a bubble of space he might fill. How would he fill it? What way would he stand or carry himself. Now take the Dr. Stockmann in *An Enemy of the People*. How would the globe differ in size now? What would be different about this character's stance and carriage?
2. Experiment with the idea of personal space. Step by step, move slowly toward someone in the class. Get as close as you can without reacting physically. Then figure out when and in what way you began to feel uncomfortable.

Even though we do our best to follow through on something like this, our bodies often give clues that we do not like invading another person's bubble. We may stiffen our bodies, turn our heads so we are not seeing eye to eye, or even lean slightly away from the other person. A character in a play would have similar reactions that would vary with the type of person he or she is.

Using Space

Moving the body on stage serves a number of purposes. It keeps a play from appearing static; it shows psychological and emotional relationships; it portrays character, and it points up the emotional content of a scene.

The movement and blocking, of course, have to fit the type of play. You would not keep rushing back and forth in *The Closing of the Mine*. Different characters move differently. Once you figure out your character's way of walking, you should know a great deal about him or her.

Staying in certain areas of the stage shows a lot about the psychological aspects of a character. One who stays toward the back of the set would appear more timid than one who plays most of the time downstage. A dominant character does not stand looking up at a platform while browbeating a weaker character, or else the action will be humorous.

Through movement and placement the audience is aware of conflict, focus, emphasis and characterization.

Exercises

1. Choose a character from one of the plays in the book. Figure out how the person is likely to move. Now walk from one side of your classroom or stage to the other, showing as much about the character as you can. Have the class tell you what they think you communicated.

2. Move in the way you think: a young child would move walking down the sidewalk alone at midnight; a man would move while carrying heavy boards on his shoulder; a person with blisters on his or her feet would move.

CHAPTER THIRTEEN
Using Your Voice

Acting can be very demanding on the voice. This means that as an actor, you need to learn to speak in a natural way without strain. You need to develop a voice that has strength and endurance and that is flexible enough to fit a variety of roles, circumstances and emotions.

Voice Production

The first step toward good vocal production is proper breathing.

Many of us breathe largely with the chest. This shallow-type breathing is OK for day-to-day life. And it is closest to the "proper" type of breathing for running or jogging when we need a quick supply of fresh oxygen, which shallow breathing fulfills.

For acting we need to breathe in a different way, to have better control of the air passing in and out of our lungs. We often tend to speak or sing "from the throat," rather than from the lungs, when we are running out of air. That means we are straining and risk losing our voices.

To produce sound the vocal folds vibrate when a column of air passes through them. It's a fairly automatic process; the vocal folds adjust as we want them to. Yet if we attempt to project our voices without breathing properly, we tense our throats; we try to "squeeze" out the sound.

To relax the tension in the throat, let your jaw drop open. Produce an "ahhh" without trying to focus or project, and don't worry about how you sound. Pay attention to how you feel, and then try to carry the relaxed feeling over to other voiced sounds. Relaxed humming also is good.

The way we breathe when we are lying down is the way we should breathe for acting on a stage. We take in larger quantities of air, filling the abdomen and the chest, inhaling and exhaling an unobstructed flow of air.

To see what this is like, lie on your back. Push as hard as you can against your abdomen with the palms of your hands. Suddenly release the abdomen, and the air should flow in. Now try the same thing standing up. Keep trying to breathe this way as you act. The more that is required in the way of vocal projection, the more control you need to have of your breathing. In a hundred-seat theatre you won't need the capacity or breath control you will in a 1500-seat amphitheatre. For an easy-going character who experiences no highs or lows of emotion, you won't need the breath control you will for an emotional role or scene. Yet to be able to play a variety of roles, you should be certain you have the capacity for doing what is necessary for the character.

One of the best ways to have good voice production is to have good posture. This way the lungs will not feel "squished" and can operate better.

You need to use your resonators to their best advantage. Resonators are those parts of the body that provide amplification for the voice, like the tubing of a brass instrument or the sounding board of a piano. They include the throat, nose and mouth, as well as the bones in the head and the chest. Their purpose is to enrich and reinforce the original tone.

The more relaxed the throat, the more pleasant and full the resonation. Tension may cause undesirable voice qualities, such as whininess or breathiness. Speaking at an improper pitch also affects resonation and can tire or damage the voice.

To determine if you are speaking at the proper pitch level, use a piano to assist in seeing how high and how low you can sing comfortably without strain. Some people, of course, will have much broader ranges than others. This should not matter as far as acting is concerned.

Count how many notes there are in your range and divide by four. A fourth of the way from the bottom should be your "habitual pitch." This means the note you hit most often in speaking. To see if that is the case, simply start to talk and sustain one of the notes rather than cutting it off. Certainly, you will not always hit the same note, nor should you try. You should be speaking within two or three notes of this particular tone.

Just as the body needs to be relaxed and warmed up, so does the voice. Many of the relaxation exercises you learned earlier help with preparing the voice for performance. When using your voice, always keep something in reserve.

Exercises

1. Stretch the jaw as much as you can, pulling it from side to side.
2. Yawn two or three times to open up the throat.
3. Exhale as sharply as you can and then let the air rush back in.

Articulation

Another aspect of voice usage is articulation, the forming of consonants using the lips, teeth, tongue, alveolar ridge, hard and soft palates and glottis.

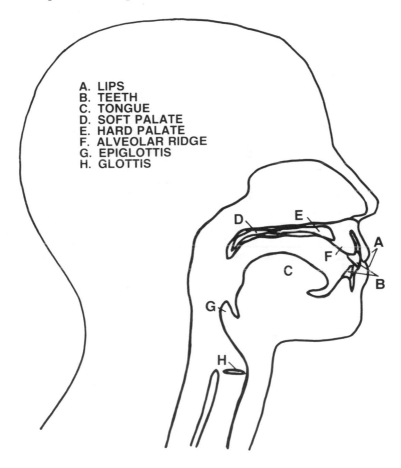

A. LIPS
B. TEETH
C. TONGUE
D. SOFT PALATE
E. HARD PALATE
F. ALVEOLAR RIDGE
G. EPIGLOTTIS
H. GLOTTIS

The way these are positioned determines the particular sound. Slight differences account for regional dialects or accents. Big differences can make a person's speech unintelligible.

You should learn to speak clearly without emphasizing the sound so much that it calls attention to itself.

You also need to be able to speak without a regional accent, unless it fits your character. The generally accepted "dialect" in the United States is called Mid-American Standard. Nearly all

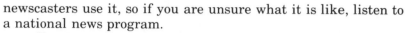

newscasters use it, so if you are unsure what it is like, listen to a national news program.

Foreigners accuse Americans of having sloppy speech habits. This means they are lazy about proper articulation. For instance, it's easier to pronounce a "d" than a "t" in words such as "letter" and "Rita."

In class try reading aloud dialog from plays in the book. Have your teacher and classmates listen for any distortions or omissions.

Voice Usage

We make many sounds that are not words. We cry, wail, hum, grunt or scream. The variety within each of these types of sounds can have any number of meanings, from rage to contentment.

Even when we use words, the manner in which we say them varies greatly, with any number of meanings. Spoken with a tremor, the sentence, "I'm going to go now," could suggest fear. Delivered with a sharp staccato tone, it could show disgust or anger. The manner of delivery often carries as much weight or more weight in communicating meaning than do the words themselves. Yet these nonverbal aspects are inexact since everyone has experienced misunderstanding or being misunderstood due to the way in which something is said.

As an actor, you need to understand the implications of every line of dialog so you can convey the meaning of the words as well as the *subtext*, the implied meaning.

The four aspects of voice usage are *time, pitch, volume* and *quality*. Time includes *rate, duration, pausing* and *rhythm*.

Timing

Rate means the overall speed with which a speech is delivered and can be measured by the number of words uttered per minute. Rate is determined by the emotional content of the material and the meaning.

You would deliver a speech that shows sadness more slowly than one that shows excitement. You would deliver a complicated speech at a slower rate than something that is easy to follow.

Duration means the length of each individual sound, and, like rate, is dependent on the emotion and on the importance of individual words. For example, if you were going to build suspense, the sounds would come more quickly than they would for a speech in which it's important for the audience to hear each word.

Duration also is a means of emphasis. Stressing words by lengthening them highlights or points out. An example would be: I'm soooo glad you're here.

When analyzing a role or a speech, you should try to determine not only the important words but the thought centers as well. This means analyzing exactly what the character is saying so you know the important words and word groups. Determining what these are not only points out what is important but can show what should be emphasized.

The effect of a word or phrase can be heightened by pausing. If actors pause before a word, they are warning the audience to pay close attention. An example, as you learned, would be a comedian's pause before delivering a punchline. Pauses also provide oral punctuation. It would be hard for an audience to follow a speech that was delivered at an even rate. On the other hand, there should not be pauses every time there is written punctuation. If there are, the speech will sound choppy.

Pausing, which also determines *phrasing*, depends on three things: the author's style, the character's style and the actor's style. It varies from situation to situation and depends on emotional and logical content.

The following could be delivered in several ways. Just two examples are shown, with one slash mark meaning a short pause and two a longer one.

WORKING MAN: Well, / I'll tell you. // My pop was an alkie. // Never amounted to a hell of a lot. // Mom / had to struggle like crazy / to keep him from beating us. / To put enough food on the table. // And she used to say: // "Oh, Sammy." / Sammy's my name. // She used to say, / "We're born into a veil of tears, and we do the best we can. // Finally, / by God's grace, / we leave the veil of tears / behind." That's what my mama said.

WORKING MAN: Well, / I'll tell you. // My pop // was an alkie. // Never amounted / to a hell of a lot. // Mom had to struggle / like crazy / to keep him from beating us. // To put / enough food / on the table. // And / she used to say: / "Oh, Sammy." / Sammy's my name. // She used to say, / "We're born / into a veil / of tears, // and we do / the best / we can. // Finally, / by God's grace, // we leave / the veil of tears / behind." // That's / what my mama said.

The last aspect of timing is *rhythm*. Any play should have an inherent rhythm or rhythms. Of course, this would be more apparent in something like Hamlet's soliloquy because it is written in iambic pentameter, the form of poetry called blank verse.

To be, or not to be—that is the question.
Whether 'tis nobler in the mind to suffer
The slings and arrows of outrageous fortune,
Or to take arms against a sea of troubles
And by opposing end them. To die, to sleep—
No more, and by a sleep to say we end
The heartache and the thousand natural shocks
That flesh is heir to. 'Tis a consummation
Devoutly to be wished. To die, to sleep,
To sleep—perchance to dream. Aye, there's the rub,
For in that sleep of death what dreams may come
When we have shuffled off this mortal coil
Must give us pause.

But rhythm, even in prose, involves such things as repeating a word, an idea or a pattern of sounds. Most comedies have a staccato rhythm and most serious drama a slower rhythm.

Volume, like rhythm, depends partly on the mood. If you are angry, you might talk more loudly or even yell. If you are feeling relaxed, you probably would talk more softly. Volume can be used to point up or to emphasize. For example, the words that you probably would emphasize through loudness in the following are italicized. What in the *world* is wrong with you? Come *here, right* now.

Volume also varies with the size of the theatre and the audience. If you're in a large theatre, your voice has to carry further.

Pitch

Another way of communicating meaning is through pitch. When you say a word or sound at a higher pitch than other words in a phrase, you call attention to it. Go back to the example at the end of the next to the last paragraph. Say the words in the two sentences at the same pitch level using only an increase in volume for emphasis. Now say the same by increasing the volume and raising the pitch. The two things work together to emphasize words and sounds.

Changes in pitch not only occur from word to w~~~ within individual words, which then is called *inflection*. ~~~ ~~~ inflection can indicate such things as a question, doubt, disbelief or shock. A falling inflection can show determination or certainty.

Quality

Quality means the changes in the overtones of a voice which result in the voice taking on a different character. Changes in quality can indicate changes in meaning, but most often show moods and feelings. For example, a gruff or husky quality may indicate an intense depth of feeling, such as sorrow, whereas a whining quality is often associated with pleading.

Exercises

1. Make a list of as many vocal qualities as you can. Then discuss with the class in what situations these would be appropriate.
2. Decide which vocal quality would be appropriate for the following sentences. Is there more than one quality that would work for each one?
   a. Oh, no! Is she going to be all right?
   b. I won! I can't believe it. I won!
   c. I'm so sorry. You'll never know how this makes me feel.
   d. Stop that this instant! I'm not going to tell you again.
   e. Aw, Mom, I don't want to go to bed.
   f. Just wait till your father gets home.
   g. I don't know when I've had such fun. Thank you very much.
3. Write a sentence of your own and then exchange with a classmate. Each of you should say the sentence aloud, using a vocal quality you think is appropriate and not your normal voice.

When experimenting with characterization, try as many variations in voice usage as you can, just so long as they are consistent with the content and the character.

and then the inflection that you think is best. For instance:

What do you mean, scaring my daughter? Just what do you mean?

Exercises

1. Go through the following speech. First, put it in your own words to make sure you understand it. Then try different ways of delivering it. Mark it for phrasing and inflection, and determine the vocal qualities and rate. Present the speech to the rest of the class. How is your interpretation different from your classmates'? Which way do you think is best? Why?

   All the world's a stage,
   And all the men and women merely players.
   They have their exits and their entrances,
   And one man in his time plays many parts,
   His acts being seven ages. At first the infant,
   Mewling[1] and puking in his nurse's arms.
   Then the whining schoolboy, with his satchel
   And shining morning face, creeping like snail
   Unwillingly to school. And then the lover,
   Sighing like furnace, with a woeful ballad
   Made to his mistress' eyebrow. Then a soldier,
   Full of strange oaths and bearded like the pard,
   Jealous in honor,[2] sudden and quick in quarrel,
   Seeking the bubble reputation[3]
   Even in the cannon's mouth. And then the justice,
   In fair round belly with good capon lined,[4]
   With eyes severe and beard of formal cut,[5]
   Full of wise saws[6] and modern instances,[7]
   And so he plays his part. The sixth age shifts
   Into the lean and slippered Pantaloon[8]

[1]whimpering
[2]sensitive about his honor
[3]fame that is gone as quickly as a bubble
[4]bribed by being presented with a fat chicken
[5]severely trimmed
[6]sayings
[7]common illustrations
[8]foolish old man of Italian comedy

With spectacles on nose and pouch on side
His youthful hose, well saved, a world too wide
For his shrunk shank, and his big manly voice,
Turning again toward childish treble, pipes
And whistles in his sound. Last scene of all,
That ends this strange eventful history,
Is second childishness and mere oblivion,
Sans teeth, sans eyes, sans taste, sans everything.

2. Through the use of inflection and variations in volume, give as many meanings as you can to the following sentences:
    a. I just love all this rain we've been having.
    b. Well, isn't that nice.
    c. You know I just want to stay home.
3. Now write out two or three sentences of your own and pass them to a classmate to present in as many ways as possible.
4. Underline the key words (those that are most important) in the following. How would you point them up?
    MAN: Oh, God, like I told someone else, I had this retail establishment. And the economy went bad, and I went bankrupt. Then this person came and asked if I'd like a job. And I said I would like a job. I didn't want to be out in the street. Not many people want to be out in the street.
4. Choose a speech from another play. Do the same thing, only make photocopies and give them to the other members of your class. Deliver the speech as they follow along. Now have them tell you what they thought of the presentation.
5. Using only your voice convey the following feelings, states of being or reactions to the rest of the class. The catch is you should do it using only nonsense syllables. Then have the class try to figure out which was which.
    a. fury
    b. a very young child
    c. excitement
    d. shock
    e. disbelief
    Now think of some others you can try for the class.
6. Quality, rate and articulation are the most important factors in determining dialect or accent. Varying one

or two of these can give you a particular accent. Leaving off the final "r" in words can be characteristic of New England or the South. Generally, southern speech has a softer quality, and a slower rate. Vary any of the three, slightly change the delivery of the vowel sounds, and you have a host of English accents.

Either through listening or library research, determine the characteristics of one of the following or any other of your choice:

    a. Irish
    b. Cockney
    c. Mexican
    d. Italian
    e. West Indian
    f. Russian
    g. Norwegian
    h. French

Practice the dialect until you are confident you can do it yourself. Use this dialect to present lines from a play to the rest of the class.

CHAPTER FOURTEEN
Analyzing Your Character

Directors deal with the overall interpretation of the play but usually leave the finer points of character analysis for the actors.

Beginning the Interpretation

To begin your interpretation of a role, you need to look for clues in the character description and the dialog. This is only the starting point. Unlike characters in a short story or novel, the characters in a play are not complete in themselves. Often playwrights allow a broad interpretation, as you see, for example, in the following character description:

CHARACTERS: MAN, 30-40; WOMAN, 25-40; MALE STU-
DENT, 18-24; LITTLE GIRL, 6-11; WORKING MAN, 25-40;
GRANDMA, 65-75; GRANDPA, 67-77; STRANGER, male or
female, 18-65.

(People of as many races as possible should make up the cast. It doesn't matter what roles they play. Even GRANDMA and GRANDPA can be of different races. Those of any age may be cast in any role. There should be no attempt at disguising their true ages.)

The idea in this play is that people are equal. It is up to you then as the actor to provide most of the interpretation of what the character is like.

To make your role believable, you need to take into consideration all the "given circumstances" of the play and how they apply to your character. Then with what you have you begin to build the role and make it your own.

Here are some of the things you need to take into consideration.

First, what do you know about the playwright? If the person lived in another time or location, how did this influence what he or she wrote? People often write about what is important to them, so understanding what this is often helps with the interpretation.

For example, if you were playing this scene, what do you think would be important for you to know about the playwright and the time in which he was writing?

1   **The Importance of Being Earnest**

2   **by Oscar Wilde**

3

4   **ALGERNON:**   And who are the people you amuse?

5   **JACK:**   *(Airily)* **Oh, neighbours, neighbours.**

6   **ALGERNON:**   Got nice neighbours in your part of Shrop-

7   shire?

8   **JACK:**   Perfectly horrid! Never speak to them.

9   **ALGERNON:**   How immensely you must amuse them!

10   *(Goes over and takes a sandwich.)* **By the way, Shrop-**

11   shire is your county, is it not?

12   **JACK:**   Eh? Shropshire? Yes, of course. Hallo! Why all

13   these cups? Why cucumber sandwiches? Why such

14   reckless extravagance in one so young? Who is

15   coming to tea?

16   **ALGERNON:**   Oh, merely Aunt Augusta and Gwendolen.

17   **JACK:**   How perfectly delightful!

18   **ALGERNON:**   Yes, that is all very well; but I am afraid

19   Aunt Augusta won't quite approve of your being here.

20   **JACK:**   May I ask why?

21   **ALGERNON:**   My dear fellow, the way you flirt with

22   Gwendolen is perfectly disgraceful. It is almost as

23   bad as the way Gwendolen flirts with you.

24   **JACK:**   I am in love with Gwendolen. I have come up to

25   town expressly to propose to her.

26   **ALGERNON:**   I thought you had come up for pleasure?

27   . . . I call that business.

28   **JACK:**   How utterly unromantic you are!

29   **ALGERNON:**   I really don't see anything romantic in

30   proposing. It is very romantic to be in love. But there

31   is nothing romantic about a definite proposal. Why,

32   one may be accepted. One usually is, I believe. Then

1   the excitement is all over. The very essence of
2   romance is uncertainty. If ever I get married, I'll
3   certainly try to forget the fact.

After learning about the playwright and the time period the next step is to figure out why the play was written, what it's central idea is. What does the playwright want to say to an audience? How is this reflected in the characters and the action?

Related to this is where and when the play occurs. Is it a modern play with a historical setting? Is it a play from a past era? Is it a contemporary setting that is different from your own environment? Are there special economic or social conditions that affect the characters in general or your character in particular? How can you make your character feel at home in the play's environment?

Next, figure out how the play is structured. What is the inciting incident? Who is the protagonist? Who or what is the antagonist? How does your character relate to either of these? How does your character contribute to the rising action and each of the minor climaxes? Where and what is the climax? How does your character fit into this?

You need to determine if the play is comic or tragic because this affects how you will play your role. As you learned, with comedy the audience does not become so involved with the character as they do in a serious play. How does this affect what you do? You need to figure out your *plot lines*, those lines of dialog that are important to the forward movement of the story. This is so you know that they are important to the audience's understanding of the play and so must in some way be pointed up or emphasized.

You need to figure out how your character interacts with the other characters? How do they feel about each other? How long have they known each other, and what sort of relationship do they have?

Learning to Know Your Character

Learning to know someone is a gradual process. You gain first impressions which sometimes are lasting but not always. It takes many meetings to know a person well. The same holds true of a character in a play. As you continue through a rehearsal period, you learn new things about a character and even change your mind about what he or she is like. Yet you need to begin analyzing the character with certain questions in mind.

You can begin with physical traits (many, of course, which will match the sort of person you are). There are two types of traits, those over which you as the actor have little control, and those which can be altered. The first part includes such things as height and weight. The second includes things like dress and hairstyle.

Here are some of the things you need to determine about the characters' backgrounds:

1. Where did they grow up? Does this affect the way they speak? How does it affect their outlook on life?
2. Were their families poor or wealthy? How did this affect them?
3. How much schooling have they had? Did they or do they like school? Why or why not?
4. What are their interests and hobbies?
5. What kind of work do they do? Are they happy with their jobs or would they rather be doing something else? Why?
6. What sort of speech patterns do they have? Is this affected by where they live or have lived? By the schooling they have had? How does their speech reflect their personalities? What is their usual vocal quality?
7. What do other people think of them? Are they likeable? Why or why not?
8. What have been the biggest influences in their lives?
9. Are they optimistic or pessimistic, introverted or extroverted?
10. What are their beliefs? Why do they believe this way?
11. Did they have happy childhoods? Good parents?
12. Are the characters good people? Why or why not?
13. What do they hope to accomplish in life? What are their main goals, both in the play and overall?

You should ask questions like this and any others you think are important in playing a role and making your character believable. A lot of them will be answered in the play's exposition.

You might want to use a character analysis sheet like the following:

Actors' Analysis Sheet

Play ───────────────────────

Playwright ─────────────────

My Character ────────────────

My Character's Background:
    A. Social

    B. Educational

    C. Geographic

    D. Family

    E. Major Influences

Interests:
    A. Jobs

    B. Hobbies

    C. Friends

    D. Other Activities

Personality Traits:

Relationship with Other Characters:

Goals:

Playwright's Life and Influences
on Writing the Play:

Play's Central Idea or Theme:

Motivations

Each character in a play has a goal he or she wants to reach.
It is something that can be expressed as an action, rather than
as an emotion or even a state of being. It cannot be anything like:
Bill wants to be respected. Or: Pamela wants to be rich and famous.
Instead, the first statement might be something like: Bill wants
to gain the respect of his classmates by being the best sophomore
class president in the history of Central High School. Or: Pamela
wants to be a top model so she can use her wealth and fame to
impress her father who ridiculed the idea that she would ever
amount to anything.

The goal does not always have to be this complicated. Maybe
it is as simple a thing as: Jerry wants to escape from the man
who is holding him prisoner.

One actor might define a character's goal in a different way
from another actor. For example, *Going Steady* is about Karen
taking an old watch from Martin and refusing to return it. She
then tells her friends that Martin let her keep the watch because

they are going steady. Late in the play the two characters have a confrontation in which Martin demands that Karen give his watch back and then leave him alone.

One actor playing Martin may explain his goal as: Martin wants to make Karen give back his watch. Another might define the goal as: Martin wants to make Karen stop bothering him.

The goal in each scene of a play might be a little different. You also need to figure out these minor goals. A character's goal overall may be to get away from a criminal who is holding him captive. Yet in the first scene the character may simply want somehow to make the criminal leave the room. In the second scene the goal may be to somehow free himself of rope used to tie him. In the third scene the goal may be to sneak to a phone and call the police so he won't be recaptured by the criminal. The minor goals, of course, contribute to the overall goal.

In the play *Are You Happy?*, the MAN has been hired to ask people if they are happy. The man's business has failed, and he needed a job. His goal might be thought of by one actor as: The man wants to find out if people are really happy. Or someone else might interpret the goal as: The man wants to earn a living. It depends on how you as an actor interpret the character's needs, wishes and motives.

The type of character the playwright chooses usually determines the situation and often the circumstances. In everyday life, a person placed in a certain situation will react differently than others in the same situation.

Exercises

1. Using the play that appears at the end of the chapter figure out one of the character's goals.
2. Figure out your character's relationship with the other character in the scene.

Determining the Dominant Traits

You need to decide which traits of your character are most important so you can portray them for an audience. For instance, with the person trying to escape from the criminal, the most important trait could be persistence or determination or desperation. You as the actor playing the role have to decide which or maybe on an entirely different trait that fits the "given circumstances." Then, of course, you need to figure out how to show this trait.

Exercises

1. Write a biography of the character whose goal you defined. Include what has been established by the playwright as well as anything else that is important and consistent with this.
2. Figure out the character's most important traits in the context of the play. Are they the same as his or her important life traits? Why or why not?
3. Work with a classmate and present a five-minute scene from the play, showing the results of what you figured out.
4. With a play of your choice or the play below, figure out everything you can about the background, physical aspects and personality of the central character. Do you think the playwright has made the person believable? What makes you think this?

Joan
by Robert Mauro

1
2
3
4 **CHARACTERS:** JOAN D'ARC, the maid of Orleans; A
5   PRIEST
6
7   **Scene 1**
8 **TIME:** May 29, 1431, the day before her execution.
9 **SETTING:** A prison cell. Shadow of bars from a small window
10   are silhouetted on the rear wall. There is a small, crude
11   table and two crude chairs. A lighted candle sits on the
12   table.
13 **AT RISE:** JOAN is sitting in one chair. A long chain runs
14   from the wall to her leg. The PRIEST stands with his back
15   to JOAN. His hands are folded in prayer.
16
17 **JOAN:** **So I am to die tomorrow?**

1   PRIEST: Yes. I fear it has been decided.
2   JOAN: I should have guessed it would be.
3   PRIEST: It is God's will.
4   JOAN: Don't blame it on God. Everybody blames
5   everything on him.
6   PRIEST: *(Turning to face her)* Are you saying then it is
7   not God's will?
8   JOAN: It is more likely the wishes of men.
9   PRIEST: Who speak for God.
10 JOAN: Who at least presume to.
11 PRIEST: *(At a loss for words)* As you say.
12 JOAN: *(After a pause)* Father?
13 PRIEST: Yes, Joan?
14 JOAN: Does is hurt to be burned at the stake?
15 PRIEST: *(Turning away from her)* Joan, must we talk of
16   that?
17 JOAN: *(She shrugs.)* I was just curious. Will I suffer much?
18   Or will I just—
19 PRIEST: *(Turning towards her)* Must we talk of this?
20 JOAN: I was just curious. OK? I've never been burned
21   at the stake before. *(She puts her hand over the candle*
22   *flame.)*
23 PRIEST: *(Pulling her hand away)* What are you doing?
24 JOAN: Just testing. As I told you, I am curious.
25 PRIEST: Too curious, I suspect. Did you burn yourself?
26 JOAN: *(Rubbing her hand)* No. It was hot though. But you
27   pulled my hand away before I was burned. Will you
28   do that tomorrow, Father?
29 PRIEST: *(Not wanting to answer)* Can we speak of more
30   pleasant things?
31 JOAN: Such as?
32 PRIEST: The weather.
33 JOAN: *(Laughing)* The . . . weather?
34 PRIEST: It is a lovely day.
35 JOAN: Yes? Really? *(She goes to Stage Left and stands on*
36   *her tiptoes.)* I cannot see out my only window. What

1   month is it?

2   PRIEST: It is May.

3   JOAN: *(Still stretching, trying to look out the high window)*

4   Oh, wait. I can see the sky. It does look quite blue.

5   PRIEST: A glorious day. You should hear the birds

6   singing.

7   JOAN: *(She stands with her arms folded.)* I fear I'll be

8   hearing plenty of doves quite soon. *(She shivers.)*

9   PRIEST: Are you cold, Joan? *(He goes to give her his cloak.)*

10   JOAN: As death. *(He stops and she goes to sit down.)* It is

11   damp and cold in here. And there are no birds

12   singing.

13   PRIEST: I fear not. *(He sits on a chair on the other side of*

14   *the table.)* Do you wish to confess your sins?

15   JOAN: I'd rather talk about the weather.

16   PRIEST: Ah, yes. Well, it is—

17   JOAN: *(Finishing for him)* A glorious day.

18   PRIEST: Truly.

19   JOAN: I used to love playing in the leaves when I was

20   a little girl. Every autumn we'd rake them into great

21   piles. Then run across the meadow and jump into

22   them. It was . . . glorious.

23   PRIEST: Yes.

24   JOAN: Did you play in the leaves when you were a little

25   child, Father?

26   PRIEST: *(He thinks.)* I imagine so. But it was so long ago.

27   Still . . . I imagine I did. I and my brothers and sisters.

28   JOAN: Were there many?

29   PRIEST: Leaves?

30   JOAN: No. Brothers and sisters.

31   PRIEST: Ah, indeed. Eight.

32   JOAN: Eight. Really? I have three brothers and one

33   sister.

34   PRIEST: All soldiers?

35   JOAN: No.

36   PRIEST: What are their names?

1   JOAN: There is Jacquemin, Pierre, Jean and my sister
2   Catherine. Catherine died as a child. What are the
3   names of your brothers and sisters?
4   PRIEST: There is Jacque, Peter, Christopher, Marie,
5   Jacqueline, Noel, Daniel and myself.
6   JOAN: A large family is so nice.
7   PRIEST: Except when we fought over the milk and the
8   bread, as children will.
9   JOAN: Yes. So where are they now? Are there anymore
10   priests in the family?
11   PRIEST: No. Just me. But my sister Jacqueline is a nun.
12   JOAN: Ah. Your mother and father must be proud.
13   PRIEST: I guess.
14   JOAN: What? They are not?
15   PRIEST: They seem happier with my brothers who are
16   soldiers.
17   JOAN: Soldiers? You mean like me? *(He nods.)* Really?
18   PRIEST: *(He nods.)* Yes. *(Whispering to her)* **My mother**
19   **thinks you are wonderful.**
20   JOAN: God bless all our mothers.
21   PRIEST: *(Blessing himself)* Truly.
22   JOAN: And your father, Father? What does he think?
23   PRIEST: *(He stands and walks to Stage Front and faces*
24   *audience.)* Not so wonderful.
25   JOAN: I see. Well, I am young. I admit to being unliked.
26   PRIEST: He says all women should—
27   JOAN: *(Finishing for him)* Have eight children, preferably
28   all soldiers?
29   PRIEST: *(Pointing at her)* Amazing! How did you guess?
30   JOAN: When you're nineteen years old and about to be
31   burned at the stake for wearing men's clothes, it isn't
32   difficult.
33   PRIEST: Yes. Well, I fear you will not go to your final
34   reward unless you confess. And dress as a woman.
35   JOAN: I dress as the soldier I am.
36   PRIEST: Then you will not confess?

1   JOAN: Confess what? That I fought for what I thought
2   was best for my country? That I led my men as best
3   I could for the glory of France and God? I will confess
4   that. But I fear that is not the confession you are
5   looking for.
6   PRIEST: No.
7   JOAN: As a result, I fear I will still be burned. *(She puts*
8   *her hand over the flame and the PRIEST takes the candle*
9   *away.)*
10   PRIEST: Stop that! It is a sin to abuse yourself in such
11   a manner.
12   JOAN: Sorry. I just don't like surprises. I wanted a taste
13   of what's in store for me tomorrow. Have they
14   decided on a time yet?
15   PRIEST: *(Shrugs.)* They don't tell me those things. It's
16   just, "Father, go hear the prisoner's confession." Or,
17   "Father, do this." Or, "Father, do that." I'm never told
18   anything about the executions.
19   JOAN: Have there been many.
20   PRIEST: You'd be surprised.
21   JOAN: I sort of doubt that. So they don't tell you much
22   either?
23   PRIEST: No. All they tell me is to pray. It's not a very
24   demanding career.
25   JOAN: Well, Father . . . *(Walks over to him, patting him on*
26   *the back)* I'm sure it's not easy listening to the
27   confessions of those who are about to be barbequed.
28   I guess most are pretty upset about the whole thing.
29   PRIEST: To say the least. It seems these days no one is
30   in a hurry to go to their final reward.
31   JOAN: Why would they be with such glorious weather?
32   PRIEST: This is true. Perhaps if it rained a bit more
33   often.
34   JOAN: Yes, perhaps. But then God does move in
35   mysterious ways.
36   PRIEST: This is true.

1 JOAN: Still, rain would at least make it seem all the more
2   apropos.
3 PRIEST: Perhaps.
4 JOAN: Nevertheless, I sort of doubt that, too. One is
5   never in a rush for the ax or the stake—rain or shine.
6 PRIEST: I would imagine so.
7 JOAN: *(She sits.)* Take it from one who knows firsthand.
8   They are not.
9 PRIEST: As you say. *(Putting the candle on the table)* **Now**
10   **no more playing with fire.**
11 JOAN: I fear I've done too much of that already.
12 PRIEST: Will you confess then and cleanse your soul of
13   this sin?
14 JOAN: Can I be honest with you, Father?
15 PRIEST: Then you will confess?
16 JOAN: I wasn't talking about confessing. What I meant
17   was I'd like to talk about my feelings about all this.
18 PRIEST: All what?
19 JOAN: This. My trial. My sentence. My execution.
20 PRIEST: Must we be morbid?
21 JOAN: It's certainly not my choice. *(She stands and paces.)*
22   But since it has been, as they say, thrust upon me,
23   *(To his face)* I'll be as morbid as I have to be to make
24   my point. OK?
25 PRIEST: *(Backing away a bit)* As you wish.
26 JOAN: *(Pacing)* As I wish? I wish I were back in that
27   lovely autumn meadow of my childhood jumping into
28   those big piles of leaves. But since that was then and
29   this is now . . . *(To his face again)* and since I'm about
30   to be barbequed, I'd like to set the record straight.
31   OK?
32 PRIEST: In the form of a confession?
33 JOAN: *No!* In the form of a protest! A diatribe! A chewing
34   out! A criticism, if you will.
35 PRIEST: If you will it.
36 JOAN: I sure do will it. *(Paces as she talks.)* First off, they

1   are not burning me out of any little problem with me
2   dressing up in men's clothes. What a laugh.
3 PRIEST: This is no laughing matter.
4 JOAN: No? Watch me. *(She laughs, then seriously)* **To**
5   continue.
6 PRIEST: Please do.
7 JOAN: I do please. I am being burned not for being
8   dressed as a man, but for having the courage to *act*
9   as one. To stand up and fight for what I felt was right,
10   for what was my duty, for what my God would have
11   me do.
12 PRIEST: You dare assume to know what God thinks?
13 JOAN: I know a lot of you men who do that and I don't
14   see any of you being barbequed for it. Most of you
15   become saints, if you know what I mean.
16 PRIEST: I think you assume too much.
17 JOAN: You might be right. But I know what my heart
18   tells me and is it not through our hearts that God
19   speaks to us? Isn't that what you all say?
20 PRIEST: Well—you also say God spoke to you in French
21   and not in English.
22 JOAN: *(She laughs ironically.)* I am French. *(She shrugs.)*
23   I guess he figured I'd catch on faster if he spoke my
24   language. Is that a sin?
25 PRIEST: Well—
26 JOAN: Well, well, well. Confess it. It is a sin to you
27   English who have captured me.
28 PRIEST: *(Whispering)* Not to me. I think—
29 JOAN: Unfortunately, it's not important what we little
30   people think, Father.
31 PRIEST: I have often heard that.
32 JOAN: So if you ask me why I am being burned
33   tomorrow, I will tell you. Do you ask?
34 PRIEST: What?
35 JOAN: Do you want to know the real reason I'm going
36   to be barbequed tomorrow?

1   PRIEST: I have this strange feeling you will tell me
2   whether or not I wish to hear it.
3   JOAN: Yes. You are right, Father. You know me well.
4   PRIEST: *(Whispering to her)* It is an honor. *(Louder)* Then
5   you will confess?
6   JOAN: *(Whispering)* To God I will. *(Louder)* Is it not your
7   lot in life to hear the final ravings of those of us who
8   are about to be *(Still louder)* barbequed for reasons
9   of state?
10   PRIEST: *(In a near whisper)* We all have our crosses to
11   bear.
12   JOAN: We do indeed. *(Puts her hand over flame again.)* Or
13   our flames.
14   PRIEST: *(Pulling candle away from her)* And still you won't
15   confess?
16   JOAN: You want my confession?
17   PRIEST: It would lighten both our hearts.
18   JOAN: *(She sits in chair.)* OK, OK. Here it is. You want to
19   take notes?
20   PRIEST: That is not necessary. It will be between you,
21   me and God.
22   JOAN: Yes. And the five guards your king has placed
23   outside my door. I guess they fear the little maid of
24   Orleans more than I thought.
25   PRIEST: *(Whispering to her)* They do.
26   JOAN: I guessed as much.
27   PRIEST: So . . .
28   JOAN: So I confess I did dress up as a man. But only
29   because they aren't in the habit of making armor for
30   women these days. Maybe someday, but not in the
31   fifteenth century. Also, I confess I did take up arms.
32   I did slay many in battle. I did wage war. I did all
33   these things. Although we never fought on Sundays.
34   PRIEST: I have heard.
35   JOAN: Sunday is God's day and I did all these things
36   for . . . *(She stops and thinks.)*

1   PRIEST: Yes . . . For whom did you do all these things,
2   Joan?
3   JOAN: You see. That's the funny thing, Father. I did them
4   for my king, my country and my God. You think I
5   made the right choice?
6   PRIEST: It is not for me to say.
7   JOAN: Right. Now everyone is mum. Mum's the word.
8   Let the girl burn. Do not stand up and defend her.
9   Do not be a man. Do not protest too loudly . . . *(In his*
10   *face)* Or at all.
11   PRIEST: I am just a priest.
12   JOAN: I am just a girl.
13   PRIEST: As you say.
14   JOAN: What does it matter what I say? Tomorrow I will
15   be barbequed and my ashes will be scattered to the
16   four winds. And that will be that for little Joan of
17   Domremy, France. Right, Father?
18   PRIEST: One can never tell. God moves in mysterious
19   ways.
20   JOAN: As you say.
21   PRIEST: So is that it?
22   JOAN: Is that what?
23   PRIEST: Your confession?
24   JOAN: If you like.
25   PRIEST: Joan, it's not for me to decide. It's for you to
26   decide.
27   JOAN: I prefer to sit and wait. I am cold and tired. I just
28   want to get it over with. I just hope everyone has a
29   good time at the barbeque tomorrow. I know I used
30   to love them. Of course, at those we were usually
31   cooking a pig and not a person, but then I suppose
32   if you were a pig you were not amused.
33   PRIEST: I would think not.
34   JOAN: Me, too. They sure squealed a lot. Guess I will too.
35   PRIEST: Joan!
36   JOAN: Sorry, sorry. I just keep thinking about those

1   flames. I'll try to think of those great piles of leaves

2   back home in Domremy, or maybe I'll think of the

3   sunshine tomorrow. I have this feeling it's going to

4   be a glorious day.

5   PRIEST: As you say.

6   JOAN: Yes. My heart tells me it will be.

7   PRIEST: *(The lights dim out and a spotlight comes up on the*

8   *PRIEST, who walks up front to stand before the audience.)*

9   After it was all over, the executioner claimed there

10   was nothing left of Joan—nothing at all, except her

11   heart. That, said the executioner, would not burn.

12   *(He shrugs.)* Who's to believe a demented, probably

13   drunken, executioner? *(He smiles, points to himself and*

14   *whispers to audience.)* Me. *(Lights dim out as the curtain*

15   *falls.)*

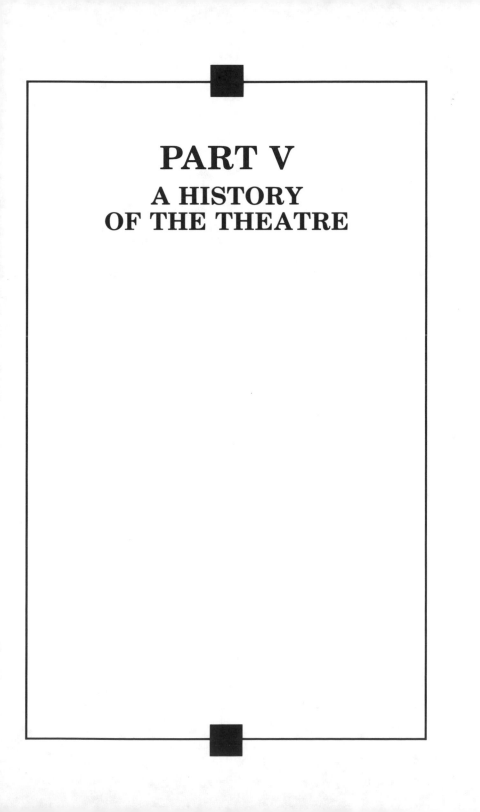

PART V
A HISTORY
OF THE THEATRE

CHAPTER FIFTEEN
A History of the Theatre

It is believed theatre began with primitive people enacting the hunt. This came about for two reasons. First, it was a way of communicating before spoken language. And the form of communication chosen was pantomime or imitation, which is one of humankind's basic instincts.

The second reason is that the imitation of the hunt changed into a form of worship. Now primitive people not only communicated what *had* happened at the hunt but what they hoped or prayed *would* happen the following day.

Ancient Greek Theatre

This prayer or worship then became a ritual. The earliest ritual of which there is record began between 800 and 600 B.C. in ancient Greece. This is the beginning of western theatre, or that which is popular in the United States and Europe.

Theatre in the east also developed as ritual but took a different path from that of western theatre. For the most part it relied more on stylized or set patterns of movement and often involved masks and singing and dancing as a part of each play.

Early Greek theatre developed from *dithyrambs*, hymns in honor of Dionysus, a god who supposedly was killed, dismembered and resurrected. Chanted by a chorus of men led by a priest, the dithyrambs presented episodes from Dionysus' life.

Later the chorus dressed as satyrs, half-goat and half-man, and the ritual became known as *tragoedia*, or goat song, from which came our word tragedy. After a time one man began to chant lines that were answered by the chorus. The first person we know about who performed a solo role was named Thespis, from whom comes our word thespian, a synonym for actor. The year was 534 B.C. when he was listed as having won the first tragedy contest.

In early Greek drama, the actor played many different roles by changing masks. The performances were not plays as we know them because there was no conflict. Even when actual plays were written, the chorus of men remained a part of them for years.

Plays were presented at three festivals in ancient Greece. They were the City Dionysia, the Lenaia and the Rural Dionysia. For each of these there was an *archon* (master of revels), who was responsible for making all the arrangements for the production of the plays. He chose which plays would be presented and their order of performance.

Another job of the archon was to choose wealthy men to help with the expense of production. Called *choregi*, they each served for one day only and paid to train the chorus, for the costumes and for the musicians, plus any other expenses. They did not pay the actors, since they were paid by the state.

When a playwright was selected to participate in a festival, he was expected to present three tragedies and a satyr play. He was also awarded a chorus. Many playwrights not only directed their own plays but appeared in them. Admission to the festivals was free, and everyone was expected to attend.

During the City Dionysia, the most important of the festivals, prisoners were released and there could be no legal proceedings. Often, visiting dignitaries attended the festival.

The festival began with a processional in which the statue of Dionysus was taken from the temple at the foot of the Acropolis to the outskirts of the city and then returned. After this dithyrambs continued to be presented, in addition to the plays that had developed. For the three days after this plays were presented.

There were three types: Satyr plays, comedies and tragedies. The tragedies and satyr plays were presented in the mornings, comedies in the afternoons. The tragedies were always trilogies, three plays tied together by including some of the same characters. Satyr plays poked fun through exaggeration at Greek myths. At the end of the festival, prizes were awarded and shared by the writers and the choregi. In later years actors also received prizes.

Many of the plays and records no longer remain. But the first playwright of note whose work survives is Aeschylus, 525 to 456 B.C. His plays relied a great deal on a 50-member chorus, although they did have a plot. He wrote about myths and Olympian law. Aeschylus' plays introduced a second actor, not to provide conflict but for variety. His work includes *The Orestian Trilogy* in which all the plays deal with revenge. The first of the three plays, *Agamemnon*, is still often produced.

Next came Sophocles, 496 to 406 B.C. Considered the greatest Greek playwright, he wrote over a hundred plays, seven of which still exist. He introduced a third actor and reduced the chorus from 50 to 12. His work is important because he was more interested in the interaction among characters than in retelling myths. His central characters are not ruled by the gods, like Aeschylus' characters, but rather are responsible for their actions. Yet they always have a *tragic flaw* which brings about their downfall.

Euripides, 480-406 B.C., was the third and last great writer of tragedy in ancient Greece. He wrote 92 plays, of which 17 tragedies and a satyr play are still in existence. The one that is produced most often is *The Trojan Women.* Euripides' plays dealt with inner conflict.

In all the plays there was a chorus, sometimes acting as a character or two characters discussing events with each other and sometimes as a messenger of bloodshed or violent death. This is because the Greeks did not believe in portraying violence on stage.

The plays were all presented out of doors on a flat space below a sloping hill. Gradually seats were added and then a *skene* (scene) building where the actors could dress and wait for their entrances. Later it became a background for the action.

One of the openings in the later skene buildings was called the *thyromata*, from which, some people believe, came our proscenium arch. The Greeks did not use much scenery, except, as is believed, painted flats leaned against the exterior walls of the scene house. Later they used *periaktoi*, tall prisms with scenery painted on all three sides. The periaktoi could be changed to show changes in location.

Various stage machines were used. Two of the most common were the *mechane*, a device for lowering and raising actors who played gods, and the *eccyclema*, a cart to bring in the actors who represented warriors killed in battle.

Unlike in later periods, actors in Greek theatre were respected and trusted as diplomats. Considered servants of Dionysus, they were exempt from military service. For each role the actors wore masks representing the type of character, like an old woman or a servant. They also wore high boots to make them seem taller.

The most important writer on theatre was Aristotle who was not a playwright but rather discussed what the theatre should be like. His book, *The Poetics*, which drew largely on the plays of Sophocles for its content, was written in 350 B.C. and contained the rules for writing tragedy.

Greek comedies were not as important as tragedies, yet they were considered necessary. The subject matter dealt with contemporary issues, rather than religion and mythology. Comedy often was political satire. There was more emphasis on the characters than the plot, and the chorus was often made up as animals, such as frogs or birds.

There was a division between Old Comedy and New Comedy. The former emphasized ideas and often had a lot of episodes that did not necessarily provide a plot. New Comedy dealt with the middle class since writers were no longer allowed to satirize government leaders.

Aristophanes, 448 to 380 B.C., was the major writer of Old Comedy. Eleven of his 40 plays still exist. Several, for example *The Birds* and *The Clouds*, are still produced. New Comedy was written by Menander, 342 to 292 B.C. It was important because it was the model for Roman Comedy.

Roman Theatre

Plays in ancient Rome were patterned on Greek drama, but the plays were not presented as worship as they had been in Greece even though shrines to gods existed in theatre buildings. The plays were strictly for entertainment. At the beginning they were presented as a part of the *ludi romani*, the Roman games which also included such things as chariot races, gladiatorial events, mock sea battles and public crucifixions.

The financing was similar to that of Greek theatre, with a magistrate receiving some money from the state. He then hired an acting company and a manager for the plays, which probably were bought outright from the writers. At first, the companies were made up of amateurs. Later there were professional companies. Admission to the plays was free.

In the beginning, Roman theatres were temporary wooden structures with a platform and scene building like those of Greece. Then in 55 B.C. the first permanent theatre was built at Pompeii. These permanent theatres became more and more elaborate. They were built on level spots with lower and deeper stages, which had trap doors for the shifting of scenery.

Scenery for comedies showed houses and streets. Some believe it was a painted background while others think it was three-dimensional.

Because the companies usually were made up of slaves, the actors began to lose prestige. The performers, known as *histriones*, most often played certain types of characters. In both comedy and tragedy they wore linen masks with attached wigs. Certain colors in costuming represented different occupations.

Whereas Greek acting is believed to be stylized, Roman acting probably was more improvisational with broad movements to fit the large theatres.

Besides comedies and tragedies, the Roman theatre presented mimes and another popular form called the Atellan farce, believed perhaps to have begun in the marketplace in the town of Atella. It included stock characters like the braggart and the miser, on whom Shakespeare modeled Shylock in *The Merchant of Venice*. The plots often involved drunkenness and trickery.

Many Greek plays were translated into Latin and presented at Roman theatres. The first was seen in 240 B.C.

The first Roman playwright of whom there is record is Gnaeus Naevius, 270 to 201 B.C. The first major playwright was Titus Maccius Plautus, 254 to 184 B.C. He adapted his plots from Menander, making some changes. Two of his best-known plays are *The Menaechmi* and *Amphitryon*, both of which deal with mistaken identity.

Another important Roman writer of comedy was Publius Tefentius Afer, 195 to 159 B.C. Known as Terence, he was a black man and a former slave. He wrote six plays, all of which still exist. He based his work on the New Comedy of Menander but tried to improve the form and structure. Each of his plays, written in everyday language, had a double plot.

Seneca, 4 B.C. to A.D. 65, is the only writer of Roman tragedy whose plays still exist. Never intended to be produced, they still greatly influenced theatre of the Renaissance. Adaptations of Greek plays, they nevertheless had a lot of violence, elaborate speeches, soliloquies and asides.

Roman plays overall did not come up to the standards of Greek plays, yet they had a great influence on later periods.

Medieval Theatre

For several hundred years after the fall of the Roman Empire, there was little in the way of theatre because of the opposition of the church. All that existed were occasional presentations of mimes and pantomimes.

Then when drama again was presented, it was part of the church service and was used to illustrate Bible stories. These little playlets were called *tropes* and were presented at Easter, Advent and Christmas. The first of which there is record is a play of three lines presented at Easter time in A.D. 925.

The plays grew longer and more elaborate and were included more and more in the church service. In the beginning, they were delivered in Latin, later in the native language of the people in churches all over Europe.

At first clergymen presented the plays. The setting consisted of "mansions" or *sedes* and an action area or *platea*. A mansion was a particular place, for instance, Christ's tomb. When the plays became longer the mansions represented various locations. The action would start at one of them and then move to the bigger acting area. Then when the action switched to a different place, the actors went to a new mansion and back to the playing area, indicating to the audience that this area now represented a new place.

In the 13th century the plays became so elaborate that they interfered with the church service and so were moved outdoors, usually to a porch on the west side of the church. The clergy still performed the roles.

By the 14th and 15th centuries secular groups, often trade guilds, became the producers. Sometimes societies were formed just to produce the plays which now were presented by lay actors, even though the church still had to approve each production.

Later plays moved to new locations, including old Roman amphitheaters or town squares. In England there were two methods of producing plays—at old amphitheaters, and using "pageant wagons" as stages. Each wagon contained several mansions.

Usually, the mansions represented heaven, earth and hell. Between hell at one end and heaven at the other were several more mansions, which became more and more elaborate. In France in 1501, for instance, there is record of a play having 67 mansions and lasting four days.

The plays were really short episodes that had no connection with each other besides the fact that they dealt with Bible stories. There was no continuing plot.

There were many special effects, such as hell billowing smoke and Christ's walking on water. Monsters, with the use of ropes and pulleys, flew back and forth in hell. Most actors wore their own clothes, although angels wore white robes with wings, and the devil had wings, horns, claws and a tail. The plays contained both comic elements and violence.

From the 14th to the middle of the 16th century the plays that had been presented in the church throughout the year were now combined into a single presentation, called a cycle play. They were still episodic, without any plots.

At first the performers were all men, but later women and children also acted. Most actors were amateurs who received only food and drink during the rehearsal and performance, although those in leading roles received high pay. Guilds or town councils hired directors who were in charge of both the actors and the technical aspects of each production. The lines, which before this had been chanted by the clergy, were delivered more naturally.

There were three important forms of drama to develop from the early church playlets. They were *mystery, miracle* and *morality* plays. The first dealt with the life of Christ, the second with the lives of saints and martyrs, and the latter with moral instruction.

The morality plays were presented from the 15th to the mid-16th century and always had a character called Everyman because he was to be a symbol for all of humanity.

Some drama also developed outside the church. Most important was the farce. A second type was the interlude, a comic play presented by traveling players usually at celebrations.

During the 16th century medieval drama began to be replaced by new forms that developed as a result of renewed interest in classical drama. Then in 1559 Queen Elizabeth I of England outlawed religious plays, which were forbidden by the church itself in the rest of Europe.

Renaissance Theatre

For most of Europe the Renaissance began with the fall of Constantinople to the Turks in 1453. Christian monks and scholars fled to Italy taking along all the manuscripts they could carry.

Italy

Italy at that time was a collection of independent states where the arts were important. The invention of the printing press also provided many more books than could be copied previously.

Since scholars all understood Latin and admired classical learning, they took an interest in the writings of Plautus, Terence and Seneca. The first plays were either translations or imitations of these three men. Of the three, Seneca was the most admired. Largely because of him, rigid rules were now written about how drama could be constructed. The writing that followed these rules was called *neoclassicism*.

The rules stated that all drama must have five acts and must be instructional. Tragedy, which could deal only with nobility, had to teach a moral lesson. Comedy had to deal with the middle classes. There could be no mixing of comic and tragic elements.

Aristotle's *Poetics* and Horace's *Art of Poetry*, written in the first century B.C., greatly influenced the writing. One rule was that all drama had to adhere to the unities of time, place, and action. This meant that a play had to occur in one day at only one location and have no subplots. Because the rules were so rigid very little good drama was written.

One of the first writers of comedy was Lodovico Ariosto, 1474 to 1533, whose two plays *Cassasaria* and *I suppositi* mark the beginning of Italian drama. Another playwright was Niccolo Machiavelli, more remembered for his political writing. His play *La Mandragola* followed the neoclassic rules but was similar to medieval farces.

Neoclassicism was too rigid to be entertaining, so several new forms developed. One was the pastoral, which contained shepherds, nymphs and fauns and dealt with romantic love. Probably the best known is *The Faithful Shepherd*, written by Giambattista Guarini in 1590.

A second form was the *intermezzi*, at first a series of short plays with singing and dancing and presented between the acts of a tragedy. Later the scenes were tied together and were often related to the neoclassic tragedy with which they appeared.

Then in the 17th century opera began to replace the *intermezzi*. It developed to add music and dance to the tragedies, which was the way the Italians believed tragedies had been presented in ancient Greece. Opera became so popular that it spread throughout Europe by 1650.

More important than the drama of the Italian Renaissance was the staging which showed a strong movement toward spectacle and special effects. This was influenced by Vitruvius who in the first century A.D. had written a book, *De Architectura*, which was about constructing buildings. Translated into Spanish in 1521, the book led another man, Sebastiana Serlio, to write *Architettura* in 1545. In this book he explained how to plan and build a theatre and how to erect and use scenery. He told how three settings could be used for all plays—tragedy, comedy, and pastoral. The first two used street scenes and the latter a country scene.

The settings, Serlio said, should combine three-dimensional elements with false perspective. The stage floor, sloped upward or raked, was to be painted in squares which became smaller and smaller toward the back. All of this was to give the illusion of distance.

Buildings, based on Roman architecture, were erected specifically for theatrical presentations. The oldest of these still in existence is the Teatro Olimpico, first used in 1585. The man who started to build it in 1580 was Andrea Palladio. He died, and his pupil Vincenzo Scamozzi completed it adding his own ideas. A second important theatre was the Teatro Farnese, built in 1618 at Parma by Giovanni Battistia. This was the first theatre to have a proscenium arch. Settings now consisted of a backdrop, borders and wings. Although the scenery appeared real, the effect could be ruined by an actor walking upstage where he dwarfed the buildings.

Scenery used modified versions of the Greek *periaktoi*, further changed by a man named Nicola Sabbattini. Stage machinery provided all sorts of spectacular effects, from buildings rising and descending through trap doors to animals and chariots flying across the stage by the use of ropes and pulleys. Professional artists painted detailed scenery. The stage was lighted with candles, often placed behind colored bottles.

Drama also took another form in Renaissance Italy. The *commedia dell'arte* was presented by professional troupes from outlines called *scenarios*. Thus the actors could improvise and adapt the material to the different towns in which they appeared. It was one of the most popular forms from the mid 15th to the mid-16th century.

It used three types of stock characters: lovers, professional types and servants. The latter two were always comic. Some of them included Pantalone, the old miser, Il Dottore, the doctor of philosophy (who mingled gibberish in with his speeches) and such servants as Polcinella, a hunchback with a hooked nose. Overall the servants were called *zanni*, from which we get our word zany.

Spanish Theatre

Because Spain was somewhat isolated from the rest of Europe, it was not influenced so much by neoclassicism and so developed a better type of drama, one that had more literary value. In fact, since so many plays were written between 1580 and 1680, this period is known as Spain's Golden Age.

Drama in Spain began to be written in the first half of the 16th century. The first playwright was Juan del Encina, who lived from about 1468 to 1537. His plays were similar to Italian pastorals. The most popular playwright of the time was Lope de Rueda who wrote comedies somewhat influenced by the *commedia dell'arte*.

Spanish drama also included *auto sacramentales*, similar to medieval cycle plays except that they used allegorical characters like the morality plays.

Plays were first produced by guilds and later by city councils.

At first they were presented in church, but later by actors who traveled around the city in pageant wagons called *carros*. The productions included singing, comic sketches and juggling. Some earlier plays dealt with religious themes with references to current events. Later plays dealt only with contemporary life. The only writer of religious drama in Madrid between 1647 and 1681 was Pedro Caldern de la Barca, who wrote more than 200 plays.

The best known and most prolific playwright was Lope de Vega, 1562 to 1635. He is believed to have written more than 1,800 plays which were suspenseful and filled with action. He drew most of his characters from historical sources and mythology. By the end of the Golden Age there were an estimated 30,000 plays written.

Most plays were presented at court theatres or in *corrales*, open courtyards formed by the walls of houses. Some scenery was used but changes in location were indicated in the dialog. The first permanent theatres were erected in 1579. In Southern Spain there were no courtyards, so plays were presented in patios.

Although considered undesirable members of society, actors were tolerated. Unlike in most other European countries, Spanish troupes contained actresses.

Elizabethan England's Theatre

Although there were traveling actors in England before the reign of Queen Elizabeth, by the 15th century they were defined under the laws as vagabonds and rogues.

Then in 1572, under Elizabeth I, a new law said that to perform actors needed a license from two justices of the peace or the patronage of a noblemen. In 1574 a Master of Revels was named to license acting companies.

A nobleman's patronage did not mean financial support, rather that he protected the troupe who then was to present entertainment for him. Actors were looked down upon particularly by the middle class. For this reason the public theatres such as the Globe and the Swan were outside of London so apprentices could not so easily sneak away from their work to attend a performance.

Playwrights were influenced by both the medieval and Renaissance theatres and by the spirit of nationalism under which the queen sought to unite the country. In fact, Elizabeth I and other nobles did a great deal in helping establish the theatre as a respectable type of entertainment for all classes. Still there was a distrust of theatre with actors sometimes being paid not to perform.

The theatre had several beginnings. First were the schools where plays, influenced by classical forms, were often read and performed in Latin. Still, they dealt with English locations and subject matter.

Another source for plays was the Inns of Court, schools for attorneys. From the upper classes, the students there were exposed to classical learning and the plays of Rome.

The third source was professional acting companies that produced plays that drew from the classics and the medieval period. But the playwrights paid little attention to the unities. For instance, Shakespeare's plays often switch time and place and have comic elements and subplots.

An early playwright, John Heywood, 1497 to 1578, developed the interlude. This was a short sketch similar to the morality play but with English characters.

Another early writer was Nicholas Udall, 1505 to 1556, whose play *Ralph Roister Doister* drew a great deal from neoclassicism. Two other writers were Thomas Sackville and Thomas Norton who wrote *Gorboduc*, the first real British tragedy and the first to be written in blank verse. The play was presented in 1561. Then came Thomas Kyd, who wrote *The Spanish Tragedy* in about 1587. This play is important because it was the first "revenge" drama, of which probably the best example is Shakespeare's *Hamlet*.

The three best and most important Elizabethan writers were Ben Jonson, Christopher Marlowe and William Shakespeare. Jonson's best known play is *Volpone, or The Fox*, a satire of greed, written in 1606. He also wrote *Every Man in His Humor*, dealing with the eccentricities of the middle class, and *Every Man Out of His Humor*, which, like his other plays, was supposed to help correct social ills.

Marlowe, sometimes called the father of English tragedy, wrote only four plays. *Tamburlaine the Great*, about 1587, was written in blank verse, the form Shakespeare used in his tragedies. Marlowe also wrote *Dr. Faustus*, based on a legend about a man who sells his soul to the devil in exchange for wealth.

Shakespeare, 1564 to 1616, is considered the greatest English playwright. Born in 1564, he was part owner of the Lord Chamberlain's Company, an acting troupe that later became the King's Men. He wrote 38 plays including comedies, tragedies and history plays.

In Elizabethan England there were two types of theatres. Public theatres, like the Globe where Shakespeare's company performed, were outdoors. Private theatres were indoors. Public

theatres operated in the summer and private theatres, which anyone who had the admission fee could attend, in the winter. The
first private theatre, Blackfriars, was built in 1567.

Private theatres could hold half or less the number of spectators as public theatres and played to a more exclusive audience.
Audiences sat in the pit (the main floor) or in galleries. The stage
was a few feet above the pit and had no proscenium arch or front
curtain.

The public theatres were much more popular and held up
to 3,000 spectators. Constructed in various shapes, the theatres
had a large unroofed pit where those paying the lowest admission
stood to watch the plays. Around the pit were galleries, which
formed the outer walls of the building. The stage projected into
the pit similar to thrust stages of modern times. Spectators often
sat on the stage.

Acting companies in the public theatres consisted of 10 to
20 men and three to five boy apprentices. The boys played the
female roles. Each actor specialized in a particular type of role,
and each playwright wrote for a particular company.

17th- and 18th-Century Theatre

In England theatre was little different at the beginning of
the 17th century from what it had been, but in other countries
there were many changes.

English Theatre

One change was that when James I assumed the throne, he
established a court theatre where plays called masques were presented. Similar to Italian intermezzi, they used elaborate settings,
designed by the court architect Inigo Jones who had learned staging methods in Italy. The masques, allegorical stories, were written by Ben Jonson.

Charles I continued the presentation of masques, now held
twice a year rather than just once. However, England was having
a great deal of inner strife. The government was overthrown by
the Puritans under Oliver Cromwell, and Charles I was executed.
The theatres were closed in 1642 and the presentation of plays
prohibited.

Still *drolls*, comic excerpts from well-known plays, were
given at fairs. William D'Avenant, a playwright and producer,
received permission from Cromwell to present an opera, *The Siege*

of Rhodes. Except for this sort of thing, England was without a theatre until Charles II was restored to the throne. From then until 1702, the Restoration Period, theatre underwent several changes.

Charles II opened two indoor theatres, and companies were again established under strict government regulation. Permission to open theatres was given to D'Avenant, who started a company called the Duke's Men, and Thomas Killegrew, who headed the King's Men. A government censor had the right to cut out anything he didn't like in the plays.

The new theatres were somewhat like those in Italy but largely like the theatres in which court masques had been presented. The actors performed in front of the scenery which was painted in perspective on drops and wings.

In the 17th century, actresses for the first time appeared on the English stage. One of the first was Nell Gwyn, who had sold oranges on the streets of London. She started acting at age 15.

Eighteenth-century English theatre is known as the actors' theatre because actors now were regarded as the most important theatrical artists, and writers received little or no money for their plays. Actors were more accepted by society, yet they still were not fully trusted. The best known actors were Charles Macklin, James Quin, Colley Cibber and Thomas Betterton.

As previously, actors specialized in the types of roles they played. Once an actor was cast in a role, he played the part as long as he stayed with the company. Older plays were directed by a stage manager and new plays by the writer.

The comedy of manners became the most important Restoration form of drama. It satirized social customs with the idea that people are far from perfect but nothing can be done about it. Another type of play written in the 1700s was heroic tragedy, written in rhymed couplets.

William Congreve is considered the most important playwright of the time. His *The Way of the World* is considered perhaps the best comedy of manners ever written.

Toward the end of the Restoration, England was becoming industrialized, with the middle class now accounting for the majority of the audiences. Queen Anne who assumed the throne near the beginning of the 18th century had no interest in art or theatre. Yet theatre continued, reflecting the changes that were taking place as the country became industrialized.

A transition writer between comedy of manners and melodrama was George Farquhar whose plays resembled comedy of manners but were more lively.

The audiences now wanted sensationalism but also felt that plays should be morally instructive. Sentimental comedy became popular. It dealt with the misfortunes of others, and the major character, who bore the misfortune with a smile, was rewarded at the end of the play. Not funny at all, the plays are called comedies only because they end happily.

Another form to develop was the burlesque farce which poked fun at other contemporary plays. The best writer of this type of play was Henry Fielding, who wrote *The Tragedy of Tragedies, or, the Life and Death of Tom Thumb the Great.* Also being presented was the pantomime, performed by John Rich. It featured music and dance as well as both serious and comic scenes and elaborate scenery and effects. Another type of play was the comic opera which poked fun at Italian opera. A good example is *The Beggar's Opera*, written in 1728 by John Gay.

Two of the major writers of the time were Oliver Goldsmith, 1730 to 1774, who wrote *She Stoops to Conquer*, meant to be funny rather than sentimental, and Richard Brinsley Sheridan, who wrote *The Rivals* and *The School for Scandal*, both of which were a return to the comedy of manners.

One of the most important theatrical figures of the 18th century was David Garrick, manager of the Drury Lane Theatre. He believed in taking control of rehearsals, something no one had done up until then. He introduced a more natural style of acting and more realistic scenery, designed by Philippe-Jacques de Loutherborg from France.

At the end of the century there was a movement toward realism.

French Theatre

The Confrérie de la Passion, organized in 1402, built a theatre called the Hôtel de Bourgogne which opened in 1548. But shortly afterwards religious plays were forbidden. Then a few theatre companies presented plays in Paris during the 16th century, but theatre had little chance to develop since civil wars divided the country from the 1560s to the 1620s.

One of the earlier troupes of importance was the King's Players, headed by France's first important theatre manager, Valleran LeComte, who rented the Hôtel de Bourgogne from 1599 to 1612. The most important early French playwright was Alexandre Hardy (1572 to 1632). He wrote for this troupe.

Although the stages resembled those described by the Italian

Serlio, the plays resembled medieval drama in that they used mansions and a general playing area.

Then Cardinal Richelieu, who came to power in 1625, helped establish a permanent theatre in France. In 1641, he built a theatre in his palace, the Palais Cardinal, which later was called the Palais Royal. The theatre, similar to those in Renaissance Italy, became the home for the company of the country's best remembered playwright, Molière.

In 1629, Richelieu also established the French Academy, where playwrights gathered to write in the neoclassic style. They felt even more strongly than the Italians that tragedy should show the results of misdeeds and comedy should ridicule. The two most important writers at the French Academy were Pierre Corneille and Jean Racine. Corneille's most successful play, *Le Cid*, is called a tragicomedy because it deals with a serious subject but ends happily. It did not follow the unities. Racine is considered the greatest French writer of classical tragedy. His best remembered play, *Phèdre*, shows the internal conflict of a woman who wants to do what is right but cannot because of circumstances.

The most remembered and perhaps best French playwright is Jean-Batiste Poquelin, called Molière, 1622 to 1673. He became an actor at age 22 and toured France. He returned to Paris in 1658 where Louis XIV gave him the right to perform at a small theatre, the Petite Bourbon, and later at the Palais Royal. Molière, considered the best comic actor of the period, wrote many of the plays in which he appeared.

The only important French playwright of the 18th century was Voltaire, 1694 to 1778. Feeling drama was too hampered by rules, he was interested in greater realism in acting and in showing violence on stage.

Despite the fact that there were no good playwrights, sentimental comedy and domestic tragedy were popular. At this time in France, as well as England, the actor was of supreme importance. Two of the more famous French performers were actress Adrienne Lecouvreur and actor Joseph Talma.

German Theatre

Until the 18th century, Germany was a loose collection of states. The country was poor, and most plays were performed by traveling companies and at court. Then actress Carolina Neuber, who headed her own company, did a lot to raise theatrical standards. She insisted on careful rehearsals, high moral standards for the troupe and the presentation of plays that had literary value.

There was also a move toward romanticism in the 18th century, inspired largely by a new-found spirit of patriotism. This came about when the government became centralized. Mainly because of the writings of Johann Friedrich Schiller, 1759-1805, often considered Germany's greatest playwright, a new type of romanticism arose. Called the *Sturm und Drang* (Storm and Stress), it was characterized by a reverence for Shakespeare, a disregard for the unities and a return to nature. Romanticists felt that there is a definite division between good and evil, that people should disregard society in order to be free, and that there should be a return to basic emotions. Schiller's *The Robbers*, written when the playwright was 19, began the move toward Romanticism in Germany.

Another playwright, Gotthold Ephraim Lessing, 1729 to 1781, was set against French neoclassicism. His *Nathan the Wise* expresses the idea that any religion is good if it is humanitarian. Johann Wolfgang von Goethe (1749 to 1832) wrote *Faust* which is considered the ultimate in romanticism. It is based on the same legend as Marlowe's *Dr. Faustus*.

By the end of the 18th century, romanticism was well-established in Germany. Other countries developed along different lines. In Italy opera was still the most popular form. Theatre was beginning to develop in northern Europe and in America as well. In Russia theatres were being opened, but there was not much worthwhile being written for the stage.

19th- and 20th-Century Theatre

Because England was not influenced by neoclassicism, it was easier for romanticism to develop. A common belief was that in order to know what is right or moral, people need only to follow their instincts.

James Sheridan Knowles, 1784 to 1862, was England's first successful romantic playwright, best remembered for *Virginius* and *The Hunchback*.

By the time romanticism became popular in France, it already was waning in England and Germany. It was established largely through the writing of Victor Hugo whose play *Hernani* was presented in 1830.

A form that grew out of romanticism was melodrama, which became popular in the 19th century. With a simple plot and lots of suspense, melodrama showed a strict division of good and evil with good always being rewarded and evil punished. The first two major writers of European melodrama were Guilbert de Pixércourt of France and August Kotzebue of Germany.

In America the most popular melodrama was the dramatization of Harriet Beecher Stowe's *Uncle Tom's Cabin*. There were several versions, but the most popular was George Aikin's adaption. Uncle Tom companies often visited a community five or six times a year.

During the 19th century theatre became extremely popular throughout Europe and the United States, with theatres for traveling companies built in even the smallest towns with a wide variety of plays being presented.

Instead of stock scenery for all plays, each play now usually had its own scenery which, along with costuming, was historically accurate. This trend began in Germany near the beginning of the century.

During the first third of the 19th century, repertory troupes were most popular. That is, one company presented a number of shows each season. Beginning in the 1830s, however, the star system was most popular. This meant that when a performer became a star, he or she often formed a company to travel the country.

By the end of the 19th century most actors were hired for specific roles in a specific play. This is when the Theatrical Syndicate came into prominence in the United States. Formed in 1896 to book touring shows, it demanded that local theatre owners work with it exclusively. If they didn't agree, the Syndicate bought rival theatres and drove them out of business. This monopoly wasn't broken until 1915.

In England actors were more widely accepted with Henry Irving, 1838 to 1905, the first actor to be knighted. He presented romantic plays and melodramas.

During the 19th century, romanticism was gradually replaced by realism, which started about midcentury in France. Those who wrote in the new style felt that society needed to be changed, and it was theatre's job to help change it. The playwright's job was to point out the evils of society so the audiences would eliminate them.

Realism was aided by technical advances including the box set, developed in 1840 and in general use by the end of the century. Gas lighting, in general use by 1840, allowed for more control. By 1880 gas was replaced by electricity in most theatres.

Realism gained popularity largely through the writings of Eugène Scribe, 1791 to 1861. He first wrote what came to be called "well-made" plays in which a problem is introduced early on and explored throughout the rest of the play.

Another popular author of these plays was Alexandre Dumas, *fils*, 1824 to 1895. His best known play is *The Lady of the Camellias*, based on a novel of the same name and better known as *Camille*. Although romantic in style, the play, written in 1849, was a move toward realism because it dealt with a social problem and attempted to teach a moral lesson. Plays that tried to teach a lesson became known as "thesis plays."

The best thesis plays were written by Norwegian playwright Henrik Ibsen, 1828 to 1906. Although his early plays were romantic, he is credited with establishing realism and naturalism. Because of this he often is referred to as the "father of modern drama."

Naturalism, first developed by the novelist 'Emile Zola, required that a writer be simply a recorder of facts, randomly beginning and ending a play, because building a plot distorted the truth. For this reason this style of writing was called "slice of life."

The most important English playwright of the late 19th and early 20th century was George Bernard Shaw, 1856 to 1950. Although his plays have social themes, they are witty and have believable characters. They include *Saint Joan, Arms and the Man* and *Androcles and the Lion.*

Also important in England were W.S. Gilbert, 1836 to 1911, and Arthur Sullivan, 1842 to 1900. They wrote operettas, for example *H.M.S. Pinafore* and *The Pirates of Penzance*, which satirized the upper classes. Another satirist was Oscar Wilde, 1856 to 1900, who wrote both novels and plays.

Several Irish writers also gained prominence. First was Sean O'Casey who wrote satiric tragedies and became known as the playwright of the Irish slums. A second important Irish playwright was John Millington Synge, whose plays, such as *Riders to the Sea*, are usually considered the best Irish plays ever written.

Russia also had two important writers during the late 19th and early 20th centuries. Anton Chekhov, 1860 to 1904, wrote about sympathetic characters defeated by circumstances. His plays include *Uncle Vanya* and *The Cherry Orchard.* Maxim Gorky, 1868 to 1936, wrote *The Lower Depths*, a play about derelicts living in a basement.

There was a move throughout the West toward carefully prepared productions, including sets and costumes that were realistic and acting that was truthful. The Duke of Saxe-Meiningen, 1826 to 1914, in what is now a part of Germany, developed the idea of ensemble acting, which means that no one actor is any more important than any other. It is the total production that counts. He believed the director should be the most important theatre artist, with complete control over the actors.

In France, André Antoine, 1858 to 1943, started the Free Theatre which produced different styles of plays but was concerned largely with naturalism. He felt that an actor's environment determined the person's movements. Because of this he took people in off the streets as actors.

In Russia, Constantin Stanislavski, 1863 to 1938, developed a style of acting that used true human emotions and experiences as a basis for feeling and understanding a role.

From all these roots theatre of the 20th century became eclectic, that is, a combination of many forms. This sort of thing was first suggested by Max Reinhardt, 1873 to 1942, who felt that each play had its own style which should be controlled by the director. Another man who used a variety of styles was the Russian Vsevolod Meyerhold, 1874 to 1942, who believed in a return to older forms such as the *commedia dell'arte* and Greek theatre. He felt actors were no more important than any other element of a production.

Important in bringing European changes in stagecraft to the United States were Robert Edmond Jones, 1887 to 1954, and Lee Simonson, 1888 to 1967. Their ideas were first exhibited by little theatre groups like the Provincetown Players who did many of Eugene O'Neill's plays, and the Group Theatre, which worked with the playwright Clifford Odets and directors Elia Kazan and Harold Clurman. The Group helped develop many actors who later gained prominence.

Other important set designers included Adolphe Appia, 1862 to 1928, and Edward Gordon Craig, 1872 to 1966. They dealt largely with creating an environment that fit each play.

At the same time theatre was becoming eclectic, symbolism developed. It used history for its subject matter and used sets that were not realistic. It is important in its influence on eclecticism. Maurice Maeterlinck, 1862 to 1949, is generally considered to be the best symbolist playwright.

Another important development was expressionism or presenting the play through the central character's eyes. Two expressionist playwrights were August Strindberg, 1849 to 1912, and George Kaiser, 1878 to 1945. Strindberg, a Swedish writer, began with realism but then influenced the beginning of expressionism. Kaiser is most remembered for his play *From Morn to Midnight*. A third writer of expressionism was the American Eugene O'Neill, who wrote in a variety of other styles as well.

Another form of drama was "epic theatre," developed by

Berthold Brecht, who did not want his audience to identify with the characters in his plays but with the issues they explored. His plays include *The Good Woman of Setzuan* and *Mother Courage and Her Children*.

In the mid-20th century Absurdist Theatre developed. The idea is that nothing is good or bad. It is only what people believe that makes it so. Among those who helped establish Absurdism were the French writers Jean-Paul Satre and Albert Camus. Absurdist playwrights included Samuel Beckett, who wrote *Waiting for Godot*, and Eugène Ionesco, who wrote such plays as *The Bald Soprano* and *Rhinoceros*.

American playwrights often combined styles. Tennessee Williams' combined realism and symbolism in *The Glass Menagerie*, and Arthur Miller has scenes that occur in the protagonist's head in the otherwise realistic *Death of a Salesman*. Another important playwright of the second half of the 20th century is Edward Albee whose play *Who's Afraid of Virginia Woolf?* is about a couple with deep emotional problems.

Although within the 20th century the United States has produced some excellent playwrights, the country's greatest contribution to world theatre was the development of the musical, started by such men as George and Ira Gershwin, Jerome Kern, Richard Rogers and Oscar Hammerstein. At first called musical comedy, this form of theatre later dealt with more serious problems in such plays as *Man of La Mancha*.

Stanislaviski's System of acting was developed and changed in the United States to become a modified version called Method Acting that relied on feeling the part. Later there were other approaches to acting by such groups as the Living Theatre, which had the goal of making drama fluid and poetic and more closely involving the audience. In Poland, Jerzy Grotowski developed a system based on total body control.

From 1970 on, there has been a great deal of speculation although not many far-reaching changes. There have been various attempts at street or guerrilla theatre, both of which attempt to bring theatre to the people rather than having people come to the theatre.

There have also been experiments with "found space" and "environmental theatre." The former means setting up an acting and audience area wherever there is space and the latter means having little separation between actor and audience.

Overall there has been more of a movement toward having plays of all nationalities produced in all countries and also the establishment of ethnic and women's companies.

ABOUT THE AUTHOR

Dr. Marsh Cassady has taught theatre at the high school and college levels for many years. He is currently a director, actor and award-winning free-lance writer. He received both his M.A. and his Ph.D. from Kent State University. He has conducted many workshops on playwriting and has directed and acted in more than 100 plays. Additionally, he has been a columnist, book reviewer, and dramatic writer for radio shows. His list of more than 20 books on various theatre arts is widely used in schools in the United States and Canada.

A NEW ANTHOLOGY OF WORLD DRAMA

*with historical introductions
to each play by*

DR. NORMAN A. BERT

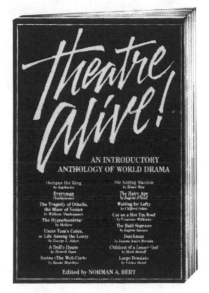

A major new anthology of world drama from many cultures. Sixteen famous plays by leading international playwrights including: **Children of a Lesser God** — *Medoff*, **Largo Desolato** — *Havel*, **The Hairy Ape** — *O'Neill*, **Cat on a Hot Tin Roof** — *Williams*, **The Bald Soprano** — *Ionesco*, **Izutsu** — *Motokiyo*, **Waiting for Lefty** — *Odets*, **A Doll's House** — *Ibsen*, **The Adding Machine** — *Rice*, **The Hypochondriac** — *Molière*, **Uncle Tom's Cabin** — *Aiken*, **Oedipus the King** — *Sophocles*, **Dutchman** — *Baraka*, **Everyman** — *Anonymous*, **The Tragedy of Othello** — *Shakespeare* and **Body Leaks** — *Terry*. All major periods of theatre from classical to contemporary 20th century. A well-researched introduction precedes each script offering fascinating historical orientation. Recommended as an exceptional text for theatre classes. It presents the entire globe of theatre history — "where we've been and where we're going." ISBN #1-56608-008-8

Paperback book (848 pages): $24.95

ORDER FORM

MERIWETHER PUBLISHING LTD.
P.O. BOX 7710
COLORADO SPRINGS, CO 80933
™ **TELEPHONE: (719) 594-4422**

Please send me the following books:

_____ **The Theatre and You #TT-B115**   **$14.95**
by Marsh Cassady
An introductory text on all aspects of theatre

_____ **Theatre Games for Young Performers**   **$12.95**
#TT-B188
by Maria C. Novelly
Improvisations and exercises for developing acting skills

_____ **Truth in Comedy #TT-B164**   **$12.95**
by Charna Halpern, Del Close and Kim "Howard" Johnson
The manual of improvisation

_____ **Winning Monologs for Young Actors #TT-B127** **$12.95**
by Peg Kehret
Honest-to-life monologs for actors

_____ **Acting Games — Improvisations and**   **$12.95**
Exercises #TT-B168
by Marsh Cassady
A textbook of theatre games and improvisations

_____ **Characters in Action #TT-B106**   **$14.95**
by Marsh Cassady
Playwriting the easy way

_____ **The Art of Storytelling #TT-B139**   **$12.95**
by Marsh Cassady
Creative ideas for preparation and performance

These and other fine Meriwether Publishing books are available at your local bookstore or direct from the publisher. Use the handy order form on this page.

NAME: _____

ORGANIZATION NAME: _____

ADDRESS: _____

CITY:_____ STATE: _____ ZIP: _____

PHONE: _____
   ☐ **Check Enclosed**
   ☐ **Visa or MasterCard #** _____
                                                        Expiration
Signature: _____ *Date:* _____
              (required for Visa/Mastercard orders)

COLORADO RESIDENTS: Please add 3% sales tax.
SHIPPING: Include $2.75 for the first book and 50¢ for each additional book ordered.

   ☐ *Please send me a copy of your complete catalog of books and plays.*